AVALANCHE ME

AVALANCHE ME

BY LESLIE ANN

Response 360° LLC

Contents

Chapter 1

Forward

People say that a person can't change, they are made the way they are made and that's all there is to it. I heard this said so many times in the working arena, usually about clientele. But I knew it wasn't true. I was a changed person and I am still changing – for the better.

This book was written for any person out there who is under the assumption that they are not good enough, not worthy to come to God. You might feel the things you've done and the life you have lived thus far is just too bad, too degrading, too wrong. I felt that way for many years before he drew me in. And then there were years as a Christian that I struggled to face him when I had transgressed. I finally learned to run toward him, not away from him even at those times. He is the only power that can separate you from your past, your sin successfully. He is the only one that can free you!

I didn't feel that I was worthy, I ran from him constantly. I have been completely set free from the past though, and I have experienced a supernatural life since! I struggled with the decision to write this book when the Holy Spirit presented it to me. I had left the bad far behind, and the good is still growing. But I could see his desire to open up these pages to you, the reader. I am writing to you, dear one. I want you to see and know just how much hope and life can be restored to you when you except his invitation. Taste and see that the Lord is good! His love endures forever! (Psalm 34:8 and Psalm 136 NIV)

I'll begin my story where it matters most, when I made the awe inspiring, amazing discovery that Christ Jesus is certainly alive! Once I tell you how it happened, how my relationship with him was forged, I'm going to take you back in time to see just how incriminating my life had gotten and why. Once we've sojourned through the past, I'll bring us back to the testimony of my faith in the supernatural power of God!

References in this book are as follows. The poems and song I've written and prophecies I've included are placed in the era that they were written or spoken, in *italics*. I will also include journal writings as a reference regarding my mindset about what occurred during the timeframe they are included, in **bold**. If it's not called out, all bible references are from the New King James translation. Lastly, in writing about my real dad, I am referring to my biological father.

When I text to others or write for myself, I capitalize any references that I make to GOD, CHRIST JESUS, HOLY SPIRIT, HE, HIM, etc., out of respect and the honor due HIS name. However, in this book I conform to the standards of publishing. Make no mistake, it's not an easy choice to diminish HIS importance in the text by doing this. But I also do not want to confuse the reader.

If my family members were to read this book, I have omitted lots of details, both good and bad. I am writing glimpses of my history; this isn't everyone's history. I won't go into anyone else's journey, unless it intertwines with my own at some point that I am referring. From cover to cover, I want this book to be a testament of what GOD CAN DO in a life given to him, after experiencing chaos without and within.

I have only one desire and that's to live out his desires for me. He is the Potter and I am the clay. He is so HOLY, INFINTE, MAJESTIC, LOVING, MERCIFUL and I have the privilege of knowing him! Whether I pray or worship, or bring a word to someone, or send an offering for another, I do it all with the greatest sense it's really for him. I'm in his faithful hands. When you know this through your relationship with him, it's quite easy to be unacknowledged. I am still relatively unknown, equally satisfied and full of joy! I get the greatest pleasure in a true, revelatory knowledge that I have been crucified with CHRIST; I no longer live, but CHRIST lives in me, and the life that I now live I live by faith in the SON of GOD! (Paraphrasing a portion of Galatians 2:20)

Chapter 2

I Came to Trust in Jesus

In my twenties I wore an impeccable façade of the latest hair, makeup and fashion. I worked for the most creative salon around, where all the stylists embraced the era of Prince and Tina Turner. I am Italian on one side and Finnish on the other, but the Scandinavian won out; I have light hair and aqua eyes. Back then I bleached my hair, wore it long, crimped and tussled the shit out of it. I wore a truly dramatic cat eye, using magenta, purple, blue, black, white colors, which I stole from the makeup inventory that I was in charge of at the salon where I worked. I did hair and makeup. I also dealt amphetamines on the side for my cousin, who was my age. This kept my weight down low. I was able to quickly shop and grab a new outfit off the rack in a size 5 after work, just so I wouldn't have to do laundry or iron for the next day.

When we went out from work, my peers and I had the attention of everybody at the bars we'd go to. I had so many guys wanting dates, that I would accept if they would take me somewhere that I'd never been before. That way I got to see a lot more fun places with little effort or expense and it bumped out the losers that didn't want to put out. I did hard drugs, drank like a fish, swore like a man, and laughed at people, being really sarcastic in humor. I didn't care who it offended because I wanted a fight.

There was this one guy in the background that I was always being drawn back to though. I was closing at the salon where I was working when we met. He came in for a late appointment, a haircut. He was tall and pro-portionally thin for his height. He said he was trying to get into modeling. I cut his hair and while I cut, he questioned me, getting to know me. He wasn't really what I went for, but it was kind of a nice conversation and he seemed interested in my answers. Most guys didn't listen much past what drink I wanted or how many lines, or did I want to leave the bar now and go have sex. The usual for fast times. So, he got to me and I accepted a date when he called a couple days later.

He used his charisma to talk me into harder drugs, then he wanted to get me into threesomes and tried to talk me into porn. That man could make me do anything though, because by this time I thought I loved him. But he was a devil, as I found out in time. We were perverted sexually but I couldn't get enough. I just wanted to be loved and held. Lying next to him, I'd think that if I could just melt into his body, I would finally hunger no more! Then he started hitting me when I wouldn't do what he wanted.

The first time it happened, I was probably like any other young lady thinking they were in love, that it was a one-time thing. He did the standard groveling that he would never do it again and I believed him. Then he'd strike out in such a flash, my mind buckled under the incredible lack of self-esteem I had. I started to believe his rhetoric that I deserved it because I was too stupid or whatever. He used stupid, fat, ugly, anything to humiliate me further when he was ignited. I wasn't those things, but by the time he really laid in the insults, I felt trapped by my surroundings.

After a couple years of abuse and struggles, while we were trying to patch things up, he stole all my money and left for Hawaii. We were both planning to move there together. He was going to be a male model and I was going to continue to do hair. He had a connection there, an old girlfriend. After not hearing from him for a couple days, I found out he had quit his job and moved out of his bachelor pad. I put it together and called that ex-girlfriend. When she answered I went right to accusations so she hung up. I immediately got a call from him in return. I was correct in my assumptions. I was also out of a lot of cash that he had no intentions of returning.

I was devasted, I couldn't work, all I could do was cry. He had been very abusive, but still I missed him. No one could help me, I was self-destructing. Even though I carried myself off as a girl that just wanted to party and have fun, inside I was so close to death and destruction it was only a matter of time before committing to it. I visualize it as broken pieces of glass falling all over, sparks igniting and flying off each broken shard.

During this timeframe when I was distraught with sadness, a petite woman with brown hair showed up quite curiously, because I don't remember how we met. She lived in the same apartment complex, and she may have come straight to my door. That day we met, she invited me into her home where she and her husband shared the love of God with me. Within days of that meeting, while I was still home in my sorrowful state, I flipped on the TV and started surfing channels aimlessly. When I came upon an evangelist's program, I stopped surfing. I don't know who he was either but his words were used to further draw me in. When he gave an invitation to receive salvation, I knew this was my chance! I was at a point of complete despair when I gave my life to Jesus at 24 years old. In my mind, it was either that or die.

I had no idea what I had done when I prayed that prayer. I had no knowledge of what a Christian life was or how to live it. I continued to live a life of chaos; drugs, alcohol, sex and vanity.

I moved in with the abusive boyfriend when he came back after burning through my money. He pleaded his love and I fell for it. But I started to see just how sick we were. One night when we were spending time with his roommates, one of them let it slip that he had bought some meth-amphetamine from me. Immediately the abusive boyfriend shot a glare my way because his roommates were part of his business! I didn't get to say a thing before his foot connected with my stomach, knocking the wind out of me. I fell to the sofa and instantly he was on top of me with a kitchen knife, yelling that he was going to kill me! One of the roommates was screaming louder than him to stop, that it would only be bad for him! He stopped short of running the blade through me that night.

I would like to tell you things got better, but it didn't for a time. I was given eyes to see that I didn't deserve to be treated that way, but I was still sick. After I got enough courage to leave that relationship for good, I went through a series of short-term relationships, eventually getting pregnant with another man's child. I was alone in it because that man was emotionally stunted too.

When the abusive guy found out I was pregnant with another man's child, he started calling with threatening messages. At that point I decided to report it to the police to stay safe. While a policeman was at my apartment taking the complaint, he called. I let the officer pick up the phone and he got an earful of the sadistic things the abusive guy had been spewing at me. The office told the abusive guy who he was, and not to call the number again. He hung up and looked at me very intently, seeing my condition and the fear in my eyes. He spoke, telling me that the city was going to take this guy to court, he was requiring a restraining order for me too, and I didn't have to do anything. He took it off me and laid out a case against that abusive ex-boyfriend himself.

You would think that would be the end, but not when it involves two individuals that were as tormented as we were. The abusive guy ended up back in my bed, convincing me once again that he could solve all my problems with our love. By willingly letting him back in, I was responsible for breaking the restraining order, I was dissolving all that the officer had done to protect me. I even went before the judge with him when his court date arrived. I tried to talk to the judge about letting him go free of consequences, but the judge wouldn't have it. He shut me down cold, told me to shut up! Then his demeanor softened as he spoke to me specifically of the cycle of abuse toward a victim. He was completely motivated to talk sense to me because he had obviously seen this before in other cases of abused women. He wanted me to get an understanding that this leads nowhere or even to death if I continued in this cycle of abuse. I cannot remember what he sentenced the guy to, but the judge's words to me did cause a wakeup call. I had enough.

I moved out of my apartment to gain some distance and tried living with my brother. I reasoned that being a man, my brother could cause this guy to think twice before pursuing me. But my brother was reluctant that I would stay clear of him. He had seen the black eyes and bruises and heard my excuses before. Staying there with my brother was short lived due to sibling issues. I was feeling a different struggle though, the baby growing inside me. I was becoming aware of my responsibility toward this other being in my belly. I had to pursue a stable life for "her."

I was long past wondering if I should abort it; I had been down that road before. My only abortion was when I was just fifteen years old. I had been told when I confirmed the pregnancy that it would be born on or about my own birthday. When I heard that, the wonderment of it all welled up in me. I was caught in the happily ever after... until I told the father. He was a cutie with a beefy car. A quiet guy that picked girls carefully, so it was a big deal in my crowd that he chose to go out with me. When we went out again, after I found out I was pregnant, we were parked in his car when I told him. He opened his mouth and basically stated a question like it was already answered: I wasn't gonna keep it, was I? I was going to get an abortion, right?

I cannot tell you how hard this hit my teenage heart. I believe it was at that moment that I started hating men. I couldn't look at him as we discussed the money arrangement. He would pay for it. He told me to arrange it and he would drive me. I think we went out one more time after the abortion. I think he was just being nice.

It was the very liberal mom of my best friend that made the appointment. She told me it was for the best as she shook her head. I felt a bit of assurance that I wasn't in it alone by telling my best friend and her mom. Money changed hands. The procedure was excruciating and I suffered. I was never going to go through it again. It wasn't until about a year later when my mom found out, that I realized just how pro-life my own mother was. She told me in tears that she would have helped me. But that wasn't a safe environment for me, so I'm not sure I would have survived the parents knowing.

The next pregnancy was while I was living a vain and demoralizing life and it almost killed me. It was an ectopic pregnancy, which can often happen after an abortion. Mine had ruptured and I was bleeding internally, but I didn't know it. I was at work when I got incredibly sick, vomiting up blood. I was told to go see a doctor by the staff nurse. I just wanted to get home and crawl into bed, but my girlfriend from work made me go to the hospital. She drove me because I was crashing, vomiting on the way and barely conscious. I was as white as the sheet I was laying on in the emergency room. The obstetrician told me I almost lost my life as several transfusions were needed.

The third was a baby that I miscarried, the father was the abuser. I went to the emergency room the morning that I knew I was miscarrying. They sent home me, my hormone levels showed I was still pregnant with an intact fetus. I was in such pain that their words were ridiculous to me. I went home knowing I was losing this baby. So, I sat in the bathtub as blood streamed down the drain with the running water. After a while I got out of the tub and laid down on the bed. All I could do was endure the labor pains and wait until I passed it because the hospital was no help. I had to pee so I went to the bathroom and that's went my baby slipped into the toilet! I was in shock, alone and all I wanted to do was rescue it. I reached for the little human body, such a tiny amount of body, and it jerked! I was totally beyond myself, not knowing what to do. In panic I flushed the toilet! Even now, I don't know how I let my baby flow into the sewer. Was it breathing? Did it feel pain? All of it was such a shock to my system, far beyond what I was able to comprehend. I had become flat out wrecked by the pain.

This was my fourth pregnancy from a man I barely knew. This child was going to have a chance at life though, no matter how hard it would be on me! I started to choose life for the sake of my baby. I stayed home as much as I could. But I was still demoralized, wanting to escape my inner pain. Once in a while I'd go out and use, alcohol mainly. Under that influence I would sometimes do risky things.

It was a snowy, very cold Minnesota night in January when I was coming home after a long night of partying. Earlier in the night I had a couple drinks, then late in the evening I had participated in a line of coke. I was comfortably buzzed. With benefits from the state, I had moved into an apartment by myself and was almost home. Right on the street in front of my apartment building I hit a slick, icy spot. My Camaro careened into a snow bank, latching its front tires up to the axle in the snow. I was lurched forward in the driver seat, causing me to hit the steering wheel with my protruding belly. I was jolted into reality and started a pleading prayer to God that my baby would be safe, not hurt by the hit to the wheel! I sat there for a few minutes begging God. I said a promise that if the baby would be okay, I wouldn't do this anymore! I wouldn't drink or do drugs while I was pregnant again!

When I got out of the car and realized that it wasn't going anywhere, I walked the rest of the way home.

I kept that promise. I became a very intent and present pregnant woman. I spent more time with my family and declined any invitation to go out. The baby grew inside. I got an ultrasound photo of the baby sucking its thumb. The doctor said it looked like a boy. I replied no, it's a girl. It had to be, I hated men and knew with a heart like that, God would not let me have a boy. It was a girl, and she is grown now. A very intelligent, high achiever in a stable marriage. In my mind, her father has always been God.

When my daughter was about nine months old, people in my life started watering the seed that had been planted when I said that prayer of salvation. I had heard about a Catholic priest and the retreats he held. Since the Catholic faith was the only minimal teaching I had as a kid, this intrigued me because I was getting really thirsty for a better life for my child. I arranged a sitter to go, lugging along the Catholic Tabletop Bible our mom bought my siblings and I for Christmas one year. It was huge, pretty funny when I look back thinking of me smiling ear to ear, that I had a Catholic Bible. I was getting snickers in return!

As the meetings progressed, the Lord moved on me one night so very dramatically. I began feeling the Holy Spirit's presence which caused me to weep uncontrollably. The looks from people seated around me made me very uncomfortable but I didn't care. I was being touched in places that had been concealed. Besides, I lived my life in a constant state of minimal comfort, so their stares at me to quiet down really meant nothing. The Spirit was going to a very deep, heavy place. That night after fifteen years, I repented like never before, for sacrificing my first child to abortion! It was in that confessional; at that very moment I experienced my first miracle. I tangibly felt a weight lift off of my chest! Since then, I have found out that the priest in my confessional was a Spirit filled believer.

I went home the same night and had another miracle. It was a very cold winter night and the chill from being out was curling my toes. I am not a fan of the winters where I am from. I have often had sleepless winter nights because I just couldn't stay warm enough. Chills would rush up my spine just as sleep was coming on, waking me up again. This night that cycle continued on and on. So, I started talking to Jesus about the night, what he had done for me, how sorry I was for my sins. Then I asked of him a very specific request; if he really had been there tonight and was as real as I now suspected, could he please make me warm so I could fall asleep. Instantly, there was a heat that ran through my whole body, beginning at the top of my head running down clear to my toes! I knew he was alive! I jumped up out of bed and dialed up my two best friends to tell them Jesus is alive! It didn't go well; it was a little past midnight. I basically got a pat on the head and told to go lay down.

Now I was searching for him! But I wouldn't meet him again for a few years. He gives me this picture of having one of my hands as he led me, and as each hurdle in life came, his angels lifted me over it by my shoulders.

Weeks later I went back to that same Catholic church for counselling. I figured if anyone could help me iron out my internal struggles, that were being magnified by motherhood, it was the church. My meeting was with the well-respected senior priest. He was very gentle spoken and cordial. But just as I started to launch into some of my heavy stuff, he fell asleep! Mind you, I was not sanctified to any sort of degree, I was totally offended! When I got up to leave, he woke up. He apologized, but I politely left. I never went back to the Catholic church and they never called me to follow up. Resentment stewed as I thought that the church was supposed to be better at helping people.

My need for Christ in my life intensified. But I would say "my child needs spirituality" like I was searching for her, because I was a tough cookie. I placed my motivation on the needs of my daughter. I tried the phone book to find churches near me. This happened a few times before I committed to go again. This one church ad always stood out to me. The ad seemed to hop out and glow each time I thought about looking again. But

I thought I was being pretty pathetic because I was so lonely.

It had been five years since praying that prayer for salvation and a lot of continued bad choices. I had a guy over that spring and while my child was asleep in her bedroom, we were smoking weed and having sex in the living room. The movie "Clean and Sober" played in the background. There could not be a more convicting scenario in my opinion than that experience! I walked by my child's room after he left and stared at her, wondering what it was going to take for me to live right for her?

I answered my own question the next morning after it plagued me all night. I settled it with people. I called that guy and told him not to call anymore, I wouldn't see him again. I also called two dealers I knocked off some extra cash with dealing speed for them. I said that I was done with drugs and dealing. Both responded with a chuckle like, okay, you'll be back. Nope. I knew my caretakers were church goers so I called to invite myself with them to their church. I shouldn't have been surprised to hear their church was the church in the phone book that I kept honing in on, but I was. After being fully informed of the church's charismatic beliefs, they were more than happy to accommodate me.

I knew the minute I walked through the doors of that church that the Spirit was there! It was the same sense of his presence that I had experienced at the Catholic retreat. I was thrilled to be in that house! I wanted as much of God as I could get! But I came with a lot of baggage and felt downright unworthy. The shame I felt inside was managed by my exterior presentation, but here even the way I looked seemed to be a detriment. Most Sundays I felt all eyes on me, and I assumed it was because of my choice of wardrobe. Or maybe it was my kid that wouldn't stay quiet no matter how much I threatened. Mostly this was in my head, dealing with fear and insecurities of the unknown.

Not long after I started going there, one of the elder's wives came over to greet me in the basement where treats were usually serviced after service. It was a typical basement; low hanging ceilings, painted brick, with little to no insulation of the exterior walls. Though it was early summer it was still chilly down there. It had a large cook's kitchen with a pass thru bar area where the treats were set out. I'd been coming to this charismatic church to search for God and truth. Down in that basement an older woman, wife of an elder, lead me through a prayer to receive the Holy Spirit.

When I told her I wanted so much to be a Christian, but I had a "whole backyard to clean up first" her reassurance convinced me I could come just as I am. She asked if she and another lady could pray with me. I gladly accepted, knowing that they held knowledge of him! As they laid hands on me, I felt the same Spirit moving on me. I said to her that I felt him, and in reply she said that's nice but I didn't have to feel anything. So, I closed my eyes intent on experiencing him regardless. I saw a dove in my mind's eye, high up on a blue background to the left of me. The dove flew down and crossed over, landing on my right shoulder. I instantly felt a peace that I'd never felt before. I'm not sure if I spoke that out, since the lady had said that feelings weren't required, I may have kept it to myself. What I did speak out was a funny language that she told me had a biblical reference. It was called speaking in tongues. I felt awakened and I closed my eyes again. I saw scales start flaking away from my eyes and falling to the ground! This time I didn't say anything to the woman. I still had too much concern about how I was being received in this new environment. But when those scales fell off, suddenly I felt his presence like I never had before. An absolute, undeniable understanding that he exists! I could not contain it so I excused myself to go home.

After some more encouraging words from the two lovely ladies, I hurried home with tears barreling up in my eyes in the car. When I burst into my apartment where I lived at the time, I walked over to the couch which was situated under a long picture window facing the front of the building. There on that couch while I cried, I stared out that window, and I spoke out loud to the air, "They don't know! They don't know that he's alive! I gotta tell them!" I just kept thinking and repeating this. I thought that if people knew, then someone would have told me! I wept and wept because if they knew, they would be as completely thrilled as I was! I just kept repeating, "I gotta tell them!"

I could not sleep because everything had changed. Everything had life now! My daughter was beyond a miracle now, she had a destiny! I knew it, I knew the God of this world was alive and had given us life!

I was like a bull in a china shop in those days, nobody was safe from my evangelistic zeal! This caused my step dad to become irate and call the church a cult. And of course, I lost friends and became even more lonely. But the miracles continued. The caretaker neighbors bought me a regular bible and I couldn't get enough. The bible glowed with life! I tried to get people to see what I was seeing. I slid that bible across the table to my sister one day and asked her if she could see it glowing. She looked at me like I had lost my mind. I got involved with every evangelistic endeavor available through the church. I also tried being a pro-life lobbyist, with firsthand knowledge of the damage that abortion does. But I was offensive to politicians because my concern was not on their sensibilities when I was rubbing elbows with them. It was on getting people to understand that abortion is killing, a modern-day sacrifice to demon gods. That did not go over too well either.

I went on a number of short-term mission trips. Because by then, God had quashed my fervency to abandon everything. I wanted to never wear make-up again or cut my hair, and go where nobody had gone, to be a pioneer missionary and bring the Good News to people who had never heard it before. He gently gave me the "big picture", as I call it. I had a child already, that he wanted me to raise here. I got it, I knew then that God has a brilliant love for all his creatures. He was not going to let my daughter fall through the cracks as I pursued my own path. But he was to be trusted that in his time, I would be able to share my passion about him.

I was so enamored at my Savior Jesus, that the more I grew in understanding the more committed I became. I can remember being convinced that if a Muslim could drop and worship their god several times a day, I could drop down on the floor and worship mine whenever I wanted to. I'd come home and get my stuff set down, then I'd drop on my knees and worship him for a few minutes right inside the front door. About two weeks after I was born into the Spirit, I read the book of Luke and found that the Spirit of God descend upon Jesus as a dove. Wow, I couldn't believe my eyes! I was born into signs and wonders when I became Spirit filled! We all are, whether we walk in that truth or not.

One night, I was laying down with my daughter in her bed. Often, I'd do this to help her fall asleep. We were both having unfettered nightmares, most likely spiritual warfare but I hadn't learned about it yet. I was drifting into sleep when I felt the Lord start to speak in my inner spirit. I became wide awake as he showed me how as humans, we are merely like ants, hustling and bustling before him. He wanted me to have a healthy fear of him as Almighty God. Then he said one word, "Tithe." With that one word I was given the full meaning of what he was saying. To tithe so he could take care of me in this world. I had no idea what tithing was until then, never even heard of it. After that I found it in the bible of course. Since that first time, he often speaks just one word and I immediately know the full weight of his meaning behind it. Sometimes I have to look up the word, and the meaning will give me more reference to what he is saying. This is one of the ways he has interacted with me. During that time, I read in the bible that his sheep hear his voice, so no one could tell me I was out of my mind! (John 10:1-16)

In worship at a Sunday morning service not long after, I experienced Jesus come in the back door of the sanctuary, walk down the aisle, walk between the back of chairs and the people in front of them, until he stood right in front of me. He reached out his hand with the palm up and spoke to me, "I want your heart." He waited there until he heard me answer him verbally, "You have my heart." He had all of me, all the mess. He started to help me make sense of why I did what I did and to change, tiny increments at a time.

Poems:

Only YOU Know
Only YOU know, only YOU do,
When my needs show, YOUR love shines true!
My life was going way too fast,
Only YOU know and no judgement was passed.
I think of where I've been, the waste,
Only YOU know, say YOU, "It's been acquired grace."
I give out a cry in shame,
Only YOU know the words to tame!
I only hope for such motherly love,
Only YOU know, giving instead YOUR love.

-

First Call
The first impression is rather grim.
What was it I was called to do?
LORD, help me to keep from comparing,
Myself to those who follow YOU,
And many of my fears fall away,
As I sit still and take in YOUR presence!
Many of the obstacles disappear.
But I need YOU LORD so very near!
Was it a whisper of quiet confidence?
Can I trust what I've perceived?

Make me sure of your direction.
Open my heart wide to YOUR plan for me,
I walk, I walk toward the prize.
I feel YOUR power inside!
Can anything stop me?
Man, this is faith!
Never let me walk off the path.
Never let me stray, I pray!

Journal Entries:

About my daughter:

The sun of a new day brightly shines into the surroundings, where a young girl is intently glaring at a morning television show. Perched on her knees, with her hands resting in her lap is the chosen position for this exercise. At the moment she is still, but in an instant this three-and-a-half-year-old could burst into perpetual motion! Her name could rightly be Action.

As she loses interest in the TV program, she is already twisting around to see what maybe of more excitement on this fine morning. When she stands up, she gives her long blonde hair a flip back over her shoulder, in a rather smirky gesture. Immediately she darts into her bedroom, reappearing in a pink dance leotard. Knowing this is probably not proper attire, she looks away, finger of one hand touching her bottom lip and her blue eyes twinkling coyly. She knows she's working me! But I love to dance with her and she knows that too, so she asks for music.

Now this modest, cozy living room has just become our dance studio! She is tall and muscular for her age. I have to guard against expecting more of her than her age, because of her stature. So when she twirls, if she hits the couch, floor or occasionally a table, there tends to be bruising. Now she pirouettes and pleas around the room, yelling above the music "Mom, watch this! Mom, did you see that?! Mom, do you remember this one?"

She is finished dancing, but she will leave her leotard on until possibly threatened. Next on her action agenda is to pull every doll sized piece of furniture into the living room for tea. As she huffs and puffs, her vocal strains for effect, you can see her little arms bulge with muscle.

This is my baby girl; she is what I changed for. The promises of GOD are Yea and Amen for me, but she has always been my incentive! Children need lots of positives to build great self-esteem. I feel strongly about this as a survivor of abusiveness. Since her birth, my emotions run deep for child victims of any kind of abuse.

About my devotion:

I love the LORD with all my heart! I want to raise my child in the way that she should go, knowing the LORD without the stumbling or the scars. I know that nothing is too difficult for HIM. As I sit at HIS feet, in HIS presence, enjoying my fellowship with HIM, HE will guide, teach and nurture me for her sake. I want to serve the LORD with my life because HE gave HIS for me!

I know the LORD has given me a heart for the people of GOD's world. I want to serve the LORD with my life, but I don't know the "rights and wrongs", the "dos and don'ts" of carrying this message that saves. I want to have the credentials so that my daughter and I both can gain acceptance in the area of mission outreach.

About my need for deliverance:

Confiding in anyone about this is disgusting. I know I have to do it though. It seems since I've taken my life and given it to JESUS, my enemy has shown no mercy so I will continue to expose him. My friend sits with me and I explain the sexual thoughts and actions I had as a youngster. How did I know about such things? I don't remember having access to this kind of information. I'm scared. I am a Christian now and I'm militant in my devotion and will. I need information to combat the sexual desires and thoughts that plague me even though I am now celibate!

Chapter 3

A Deeper Dive

My folks did not know how to parent, my mom was young herself. We are twenty years apart and she already had my sister before me. My three siblings, from marriage to my real dad, are all about two and a half years apart in age. There is my older sister, then me and next my brother. We also have a half-sister eight years younger than me, by my step-dad. When my mom was divorced from my real dad, she may have been a bit self-occupied, I don't know. She divorced my real dad when I was barely old enough to walk, so I don't know just how to describe her state of mind then. I know that her marriages were full of drama, and she also was very narcissistic when I was older.

I was born in the iron mining region of Minnesota. Shortly after my mom and dad married, the mining of iron ore dried up, leaving the area my folks were from in a depressed climate. They moved to the Twin Cities for better employment. I lived in the suburbs of Minneapolis until I left the state. Everyone has heard of our winters, but I enjoyed our four distinct seasons and our large lakes!

I am an artistic sort, feeling like I could try anything at least once. I basically settled on painting with acrylics, first on canvas and then pretty much anything with the advent of chalk paint. I've always written but never consistently. As a child, there was absolutely no prodding of future destiny for me. The best I ever got was a birthday present from my mom when I was thirteen, I think. It was a brown crossbody purse. Inside was a pencil and a small flip open notepad. I looked at her curiously and she said, "You want to be a writer, don't you? Well, writers take notes." Yes, I replied, in shock that she even remembered I had expressed that. That was it, no other nurturing about a future.

We lived in a duplex when my mom and real dad divorced, so my mom stayed there awhile after. She would let my older sister and I out to play. She told my sister, who was probably just under five, to watch me. Well, my sister didn't want to. She was faster without me, following behind and running after her neighborhood friend. So, she would leave me in her dust. I was left alone as a toddler for the monster to find. I remember going into the duplex next door with the teenage boy. I vaguely remember playing "doctor."

I ever so slightly remember being coached not to tell anybody. And then I was scooted out the door, like a puppy let out to pee. This was confirmed to me as an adult by my older sister. She said that one time she saw me come out of that door. I don't know how many times it happened.

Immediately I was ashamed and angry, too young to express what had happened to me. It came out in an over stimulated personality, lashing out and then in great fear and tears. I sucked my thumb, wet myself and the bed a lot, hid so nobody could find me. One day my mom started looking for me to feed us dinner. When I couldn't be found she called her friends to come and help look for me. Hours passed as I watch this from behind the couch. I wet myself and sucked my thumb until somebody finally looked there. I was yelled at, spanked and sent to bed without any food.

The enemy of my soul was able to take me hostage at a very, very young age. What went on behind those walls next door caused me shame, fear, isolation, blame, suicidal tendencies, repeat nightmares and a split personality. Those were my demons and I collected them as I grew up. This is also when it started, between my mom and I. She was supposed to parent me, love me. But she thought that as an obedient child I was supposed to make her life easier. She began to disassociate with me in a subtle but real way. And I picked up on it because I was in such need of moral support.

I was also born with really high functioning senses of smell, hearing, touch and taste. I had a strong sense of intuition too, prior to knowing my gifts from God. But as I started to sense my mom's dislike for me, at a very young age I lashed out in retaliation. I would reject her kiss good night and I became really sassy. By the time I was six, she openly disliked me and I was always trying to find where I fit in.

We moved by the time I was five and the new neighbors we had were nice. I would just drift over and the lady of the house would invite me in and talk to me. Her kids were boys, so she really was just being nice. My mom resisted their attempts to be kind. When my mom would tell my sister to keep an eye on me, my sister would still just let me roam. My mom told me to stay in my own yard. But I liked the tall sun flowers that were growing in their backyard, so I was always going over there. Decades later my mom admitted to me she didn't love me back then.

When my mom was dating my step dad, he was nice to us, but after they married that changed. He was really intolerant of us. He wouldn't let us sleep in on Saturdays, he'd come into the bedroom and yell, "Get out of bed you lazy assholes!" He would hit us across the face if we pissed him off. When I was in junior high, I got suspended twice for telling teachers to f*** off.

The last time I did that, my mom had to come and get me. We were sitting at the kitchen table when she told me that my dad knew. Because he was so abusive, she would sometimes cover. But not for me, not this time. He came in the back door right then. He walked over to the table between us with a look of hazard on his face and said, "What's this I hear?" My mom responded and told him again what I did. He back handed me across the face and my head hit the wall behind the chair and I saw stars. My mom burst into tears. Tears welled up in my eyes and I teetered for a moment between consciousness and black out. Then I just walked to my room as he started yelling that I was grounded or something. I was learning to tolerate the pain.

One time my step dad kicked my brother as he laid on the living room floor with a broken arm, for taking his fishing gear without asking. My brother was riding his bike home from fishing that day, when a van passed him and the van mirror clipped his elbow, sending him into a ditch on the bike. The tackle box flew and his arm needed surgery. No sympathy from my dad though, he kicked that "dog" while he was down. I remember cowering in the very front of the house outside the coat closet with my brother once, because my dad was on a war path and looking for us. Fear was a constant emotion in my childhood. My life was chaos and dysfunction as I was growing up.

When I was around seven or eight, we moved into a new house, the first on the street. I started stealing cigarettes from my mom's pack. I'd go out to the field across the street where I learned to smoke. I liked the fire that the matches produced, so I started small field fires. I was always able to put them out, luckily.

Around this time, my mom started sending us to visit her mom, for one week, separately. This was probably for her sake, though my sister liked going. I was upset about going because I knew my grandma shared my mom's feeling of dispassion towards me.

We were playing in the backyard at grandma's house, when I was a bit younger. We would run and take a big jump onto a ceramic planter pot, then grab the window sill and climb up to the clothes line pole to swing with our hands. When it was my turn, my sneaker slipped on the shiny planter pot and I fell off of it, hitting my head on it. It knocked me out. When I came to, I was laying in my mom's lap as she poured peroxide into this gaping wound on my head. I saw the blood on the towel my mom was using. My grandma just stood there watching. No urgency, no run to the hospital. Years later when we were adults, my sister called me about that incident too. She said she witnessed an angel in the yard the day I fell and cracked open my head. I think if that angel hadn't been there, I probably would have died.

I was sent there for a week this time; while my grandpa was at work we went shopping. My grandma told me she would buy me an outfit like she had for my older sister. She said I better not get my hopes up that it will be as nice as my sister's because she liked her more. When my eyes filled up with tears, she told me not to make a scene or she would leave and I wouldn't get anything. When we got back to my grandma's house, I went up to the room I stayed in. I slid under the bed with a book of matches. I started lighting them and noticed the shears on her windows. I touched the lit match to the shear, watching with amazement how the flame traveled up so quickly. I blew and it was out. I tried it again with a match I had blown out and it still traveled, but not as much. I did this a few times, the sheers were toast.

When it was time for dinner, my grandma came looking for me. She opened the door and gasped! She slammed the door and went downstairs. I was in that room alone for hours, and then my mom came in. She had driven three hours to get me because apparently my grandma called her and told her to. Quietly she packed my bag and we left. It was a funny ride home; my mom was actually empathetic to a point. I was able to tell her what my grandma said. We didn't talk for most of the ride but she never yelled and she didn't tell my dad.

I was around eleven when I started cutting myself, but there was no term for it then. I was only trying to get up the nerve to slice deeper, to cut a vein. I wanted to kill myself. I'd go in the garage, after a chaotic scene inside the house. I had such hatred steaming in me, I hated everyone in that house! I was using food now to give me some satisfaction, so I became the fat one that they all chided. I was well aware of the disregard my mom had for me now, and constantly clashed with her to get even. I hated my older sister back then because she had all my mom's positive attention, as did my baby sister. And since he was a boy, my brother was showered with sports gear for whatever sport he was into at the time. This was the way my mom leveled out her guilt over my step dad's constant abuse of my brother. Apparently, my brother reminded him too much of my real dad.

On weekends, getting out of the house was always a priority after my chores were completed. One Saturday, I took a walk up to the nursing home where my grandma was now living. My mom told me to go visit her so reluctantly I did. My mom had moved her closer after my grandpa had died. By this time, she had either dementia or Alzheimer's. As I sat with her, she said nothing, just stared. I was eleven and it was the last time I went to see her.

On the way home, I decided to walk through neighborhoods instead of taking a straight path home so I could burn more time away. I walked past an old Ford Model T in the yard of a house. I was looking at the car when I noticed a guy out back of the car washing it. I recognized him, he was a high schooler. He was cute, and nice because he invited me up to see the car and talked to me about school. He was home alone so he invited me in to get something to drink. Then he invited me into his bedroom to see something. Then he forced himself on me as I shouted at him to get off of me. Then he raped me. After he got off of me the scarf that I was wearing in my hair had slid down on my face. I straightened my hair and pulled up my pants. He acted like nothing had happened and his words were cruel. I was in a state of unbelief, so I dazedly left the house and started the walk home. I still see it in my memory as a very surreal, dazed walk home. I didn't tell anyone; I just felt more shame.

The following year, I dropped a bunch of weight, got interested in boys and drugs. The rest of those years through junior high and high school were about getting the guy who had the best drugs. I got pretty good at it too, because as I lost weight I became very pretty. Even my girlfriends used me though. I was the bait to bring the guys around. I got my pick and they got the rest.

I didn't really worry about school because most of that time I was able to keep my head above water without much effort. I was smart. By senior high I didn't care anymore so I skipped a majority of it. I didn't have the credits to graduate either so I quit. But I wanted to get a real job to earn enough for rent so I got my GED. I was also given an IQ test. I scored very high. Apparently, my real dad was very intelligent as well, borderline genius. I always said there is a fine line between genius and madness. He drank himself to death, choosing to drink instead of living sober and wishing he had a drink every day of his life. That was his mentality.

My best buddy from high school days was a man that worshipped me, and of course he was just not my type. I think he would have bought me two worlds! He loved me enough to rescue me out of any messed-up hole I found myself in. He saw me do terrible things and he still loved me. He was the one I felt safe enough with to experiment with needles. However, he almost overdosed me once. It was an experience I will not forget, as I felt my life's energy flowing out of my body. By quickly shooting me with amphetamines I didn't overdose. Later in life I led him to Jesus. That was a very happy experience! He died only a few years later.

When I was sixteen, after going to court for truancy and having the judge rule me as "Incorrigible", my mom signed legal custody over to a neighbor lady that I babysat for. This lady liked me and she was my "To Sir, With Love!" If you have not seen that movie, you should. This lady taught me how to grace a room, dine with charm, dress correctly for the occasion and so much more. But she also used me to watch her two children below four years old. The reason she took charge of me was that I could stay over now and watch the kids 24/7 if need be. She was divorced and breaking into real estate so her hours were long, then she would go out after. I didn't care because she let me go out when I wasn't sitting. My situation with this lady only lasted about a year and a half. This lady also met her future husband during that time and he was not my fan. He gave me an ultimatum one night, to straighten up or leave. I was 17 when I moved out.

When I first started living with her though, I was scarred by the fact that my family was only a block away and I was no longer welcome. I went through that first Thanksgiving alone, because this lady had taken her kids with her to her parent's home up north. I kept looking out the window at my house, wondering what they were doing, knowing they were eating dinner together. I was suicidal by the end of that day. But it caused a great resolve in me that I could get through any 24-hour period regardless of what day it was on the calendar.

I got a great job when I was 17, with a young woman I had met out in a bar. Her home life was bad too. We lied our age and applied together for a factory job. The HR representative called us both in after we filled out our applications. As we were seated together in front of his desk, he walked around it to situate himself between us and leaned against his desk. He looked at both of us rather carefully. I was more rebellious than my friend, so I was ready to bolt out the door first, if he was going to catch us in our lie. But then he touched my knee, and said, "You're both hired." That was my first job. That job is how I was able to buy my first car, a brand new Z28 Camaro, bumblebee yellow with racing stripes.

I bounced around, living place to place while I was that young. I didn't want to abide by any authority, so when there were roommate rules, I would just ignore them. I ended up being kicked out of a number of places for this. Eventually I totaled the car, drunk and high on drugs. The night I did, I had left a friend's house with no destination. At a stop sign, I decided to put the pedal to the floorboard and see what I ended up with, preferring death. I bounced off cars and the median until I hit a vehicle with enough force to stop my acceleration. First responders found a pulse, so off to the hospital I went. I wasn't treated very nicely there because the emergency room doctor didn't like that I was so intoxicated, so he kept hitting my chest to get me revived. I don't really recall much more of that night. But it garnered some sympathy from my mom and she allowed me to move home, into the basement for cash.

When I couldn't stand our interactions any longer, I moved out into my own apartment. It wasn't easy to pay my rent, I had lost my factory job over my excessive sick leave. I managed to find a cocktail waitress job at a very busy nightclub, attached to a rowdy bar. I served drinks on the bar side. I would ride the bus to my job and hope for a ride home since it was always later than buses traveled. I got so many dates and offers there that it wasn't a problem usually. Not enough money to eat and pay rent though.

I would talk to certain regulars at the bar about life. I got to know many of them personally. One asked me to go out with him and he would pay my rent. I was certainly naïve because I accepted without much thought. On this date, he took me to his place where he cooked for me. But then he wanted more, like a bath together, then sex. I did what he wanted, even though I was not the least bit attracted to him, because I needed the rent. He gave me the money afterward and I felt like a whore. I never did that again.

This event made me realize just how much the other sex wanted to use me, yet I went out with them and let them use me. I was a paradox. I didn't know it had a spiritual component. All I knew was how much I hated myself for it all.

One regular guy at the bar was so tall and generous with me, always insisting on giving me a ride home. It was easy to let it become something else. I started to really have feelings for him. Once, after we had sex, we were engaged in pillow talk. I spoke about how I wanted to be married and have kids, just like a normal lifestyle. He chuckled and said, "You?! Who would wanna marry you? You're a slut. I mean you're great in bed. But nobody wants that kind of girl to bring home to their mother. Get real!" My inner soul burned with hatred toward him! I made a pact with myself then and there, that I would get really good at what they wanted and use them for anything and everything, like they used me.

I got very good at what they wanted – sex. In return I got good drugs, exciting dates, an occasional trip, but couldn't deny it was crafty. The hurts never stopped coming though. If I didn't want to do something for them, they quickly turned the table, calling me a slut. So, for years I stayed in my lane. As I matured, I became very pretty and had no lack of male suitors. I didn't believe I was pretty no matter how many times I heard it. I was engaged four times. The longest I stayed in a relationship was about a year. I didn't believe any-thing anyone said to me, I had zero trust, zero self-confidence so relationships never worked.

Insecurities ate at me constantly. I had a lifelong nail-biting habit too. And in my sleep, I still sucked my thumb! From sucking my thumb, my front teeth were crowding, I was born with some of that too. I hated my teeth though. I had a motto, that if runway models didn't smile, I didn't need to either. But I heard a lot of comments about it, "You're so pretty, you should smile more." I heard it a lot, everywhere I went it seemed.

Whatever, I thought, I was doing pretty good the way I was. When I got ready to go out, by doing make-up and hair, and dressing incredibly posh, I felt myself change. I was now sexy, full of confidence and swagger. But once the fun was done, I was back to being pathetic me. I saw my life like a tunnel with no light showing the way out. I was a seriously screwed up human being.

I applied for grant money, eventually receiving enough aid to enroll in Cosmetology school. I was good at it and got special favors from the instructors. They were also aware that I was stealing supplies from the school and other students. A couple older students and instructors gave me sympathy, knowing some of my background. As a whole though, the class definitely hated me. I finished as fast as possible and started my career in a tiny salon not far from home, within walking distance. It became my happy place.

Poems:

-

Inward Secret
Did you see me on the road?
Or were you glancing right through me?
Did you know I carry a heavy load?
I saw you; I couldn't help my staring.

I stopped trying to gain approval,
It hurts to not be known by you.
I wonder always about you,
Even dreams of clandestine conversations.
Let it go, let it go.

-

<u>Untitled</u>
Inside I see what my heart is telling me.
I see a wall – come down, avalanche me!
I want to be considerate and free,
I don't want to listen to what I'm telling me.

Chapter 4

The Residual Effect

After my infilling with the power of the Holy Spirit, I started to question some of my "natural" tendencies; fear, paranoia, anxiety. And those nightmares both my daughter and I were struggling with on the same nights were also telling signs of deeper issues. Being advised by an older believer in the church who recognized my need for spiritual deliverance, I decided once again to seek counseling to be a better parent. I also took Spiritual Warfare classes through my new church.

My quest was for truth now, all the unseen things were very real to me. I wanted to know what I had opened myself up to as I walked in the depth of sin I was saved out of. Really there is no way to describe my sense that there were forces against me, except through the amount of deliverance that started to occur. I knew that I had met the holy supernatural, but what I didn't understand was how the unholy spirits operate in our lives. I was now completely aware of them though.

I learned through the Spiritual Warfare classes that certain habits can be symptoms of demonization. And yes, I'm living proof that deliverance may be needed after conversion. At that time, this was a controversy, but I know what I experienced. After certain classes, I'd go home and pray about how the lesson impacted me and what was needed for me to do. I'd pray in tongues and worship by singing out loud.

Once after this worship time, the Holy Spirit took over. I felt deep within my gut a revulsion stemming up, brimming over into a gasp or a loud huff, not once but several times. There was even a change in the atmosphere, as demonic entities left me. I was taught what to say, so I spoke out to leave my place and I prayerfully covered the doorposts and windows with the precious blood of Jesus! As I added understanding, more deliverance would happen over those early days.

As I became freer, I would enter into what I now know as intercessory prayer. Intercession is a type of prayer, usually in tongues. By obeying this unction, the Lord is now able to set forth his desires in the earth realm. It's like we are activating his will in the earth. We may not fully understand the prayer ourselves. The

Holy Spirit is working through us to accomplish God's will. He doesn't act alone; he calls us to participate with him.

I started seeing a picture in my mind's eye of what this function of intercession is like. I would see it as bowls of God's desires in the form of liquid fire in each outstretched hand, poured out as we exhaust ourselves in intercessory prayer. During intercession, I would often not know what I was praying, as my heavenly language was being employed. I gave myself to it and the Spirit would pray through me.

I also experienced physical impressions when I would intercede. While praying for my brother once, I felt a tightness around my midsection, so tight it was choking off emotions and causing pain. I felt this tightness for days and saw it, like a big linked chain. As I exhausted my call to intercede for him, I felt the chain break and I knew I was finished. I took the opportunity later to ask my brother if he had been experiencing pain from a tightness in his midsection, and he did confirm it had been an issue. He described it as stomach pain.

Often, out of experiences at church when truth was revealed through a teacher or special speaker, I would be given understanding for myself. The Spirit would speak to my inner being, showing me what it was that I happened to be dealing with, and instructed me how to pray.

At a women's retreat once, I could not stay seated. I was perplexed about what in the world had me so agitated. I prayed earnestly that weekend because I didn't want to be different from these free-spirited women that I found so appealing. A couple of times I just had to go find a place off by myself. I needed to hear from the Lord exactly what was going on with me!

That small voice inside of me spoke as I sat on a picnic table. He showed me how all those years ago when I was molested as a small child, my mind fractured. He explained that this is a mechanism of his design, to save a victim from shear panic and terror. I'm going to include what I wrote after the fact here, as it relates better what I was shown. However, at present it is coming forth that our brains are wired to protect our mind in this manner. God is good!

Journal Entries:

For my child:
This is for my daughter, though she is young I know she is intelligent and she knows the negative effects of what I endured. Here's the truth about the abuses, GOD's defenses and the truth about splits.

It seems so weird how the day can be just beaming with sunlight, warm and fresh. But life, or the person living it is torn, broken, beaten, near defeat. Over the same thing that happened years ago, but has affected life ever since. Today it was reaffirmed, I'm a bitch, nobody likes me because I'm such a bitch. "What is that church doing for you anyway? (It's healing.) Teaching you to be a bitch?! You don't need a church; you need a psychiatrist!" Finally, I reply that now I know what I can expect from the very people who are supposed to love me, I can't expect that love. This assault is a trigger.

Splits unmasked:
So much happened at this retreat. I thought I had been hanging too far away from GOD to be shown anything. I haven't been in HIS presence in weeks. I'm not making the connection. I didn't have to, HE did! We were into a worship service and I felt HIM gently say in my spirit that I hadn't trusted HIM enough to be everything HE wanted to be to me. HE told me why I didn't trust HIM enough. This was interesting since not only were my friend and I discussing that it takes whole trust to follow the SPIRIT into the deepest relationship, but I had trusted that HE now was my Daddy – I had never called anyone Daddy before, My Savior, My LORD! But HE said I had not trusted HIM as my HUSBAND.

Then the meeting progressed and a word about fear was brought forth. It was meant to empower, I wanted to be empowered. But something made me want out of that room; I was gone. In my dorm I broke a little. "Tell me what YOU want from me!" I already knew – HE wanted full access.

I went to shower, I needed to be clean. I always felt more human after a shower, I needed to be clean! By then the sermon was over and women were coming in and out. I coaxed a friend to go outside. As I told her what is going on in me, at the same time GOD was revealing to me, helping me to discover just who was speaking here.

The Lord revealed a rebellious, controlling, manipulative young woman who just wants to have fun. She can get anybody to go with her because she knows how to escape. But this time she can't escape because the LORD is revealing her, with the intent of restoring the whole person to me. I am realizing all this and I just break down crying, because this "split" is realizing WHO she has been running from, and there is no place to run! HE has revealed her and she is a part of me and we are HIS. HE loves me, all of me, HE has freed me. This is just another symptom of a sinister abuse. But GOD is so thorough and today I have identified a split, one which I have been dealing with for a very long time. I've been given peace about this confusion; why I am the way I am when I don't want to live as a victim. But I didn't understand why I acted out when I didn't want to.

Healing has been deep and I praise GOD for the comfort that let me trust HIM enough to go really deep. It's pain though, but I trust HIM to go unlock the dark "drawers" of my mind. HE showed me, HE possesses the "keys" to the drawers and unlocks them, exposing the darkness. If I could describe the sense of emotional pain in physical terms, it's graphic – like surgically cutting me from my throat to my pelvic and laying it open to bleed. The pain is so intense, the emotional response so overwhelming, I am physically exhausted after. I usually go to sleep, but a good, healing sleep. I have come to find that when I go there with HIM, I am made more whole than I was before we went there each time.

These drawers are actually where my splits have retreated. I was amazed when it first happened. One drawer exposed, out of my anguish came the voice of a very small child yelling, "No, No! Don't do it, don't do it! Oh my, oh my oh my!" Then came screams from this small girl that had been suppressed for a very long time. That's why I chose to let GOD take me there. HE needs to empty me of the darkness where the wounds are hiding and fill it up with HIMSELF. GOD is love!

But it is still a choice to go there, and sometimes I am just not strong enough to endure what it takes. HE is never pushy, I have a choice, HE is gentle. Everything about the abuse that I was in bondage to has been revealed to me through letting GOD take me there, via the HOLY SPIRIT.

If I really believe that GOD made me, I mean really created my mind, body and emotions, then isn't it a part of GOD's design in a person to create the defenses of the mind? Just as HE created immunities for the body, I believe GOD created my mind in such a way that when horrific things were put upon me at a very young, defenseless age, this defense was put into action. It helped this young child break off and away from the reality, splitting into the dark drawers of asylum.

By the time I gave my heart to Jesus, my mind was so inundated by conflicting spirits, I would be confident and savvy one minute, then skyrocket down to the very depths of despair the next. I saw no foothold to rest on to gain any strength, it was a topsy turvy existence. It was quite exhausting and my only way of handling this inner turmoil was to masquerade with different faces. I got good at pretending.

Fear was a binding force for me as a young believer. Once in the church arena, I met young men that found me attractive and asked to see me. However, I had a problem with trusting men, given the extent that I had been used and abused. One man who was extremely handsome, articulate and full of faith, started dating me. On a long walk together, I told him that I didn't trust men. After that walk, he never called me again. That was a deal breaker for him.

If a relationship did take root, it was usually quashed by something I did, like a tantrum of sorts or too heavy petting. We all strived for purity, at least those I hung out with did. But for many years, I was my own worst enemy until I found I needed deliverance from these types of demonic culprits. There were sexual sins that I consented to that needed repenting of, so that the Lord could deal with it and take me further to freedom.

I began to structure my words in prayers of repentance to divinely cover areas of omission and commission – granting authority when I didn't understand I was allowing it (Ephesians 5:8-17). This would give the Lord legal access over the issue, for my benefit of healing and deliverance. As time went on, I became much more peaceful in my own skin. If I felt overwhelmed, I would isolate and pray. I did this in all areas of my life that were out of sorts, all relationship issues.

God showed me how unrealistic it was to expect others to know what I wanted or needed if I wasn't able to vocalize it. In other words, he taught me how to articulate my inner thoughts or needs in a relationship.

This was overcoming the fear of rejection in me, from years of battling for my place in my family structure. I had to overcome feelings that my thoughts held legitimacy. He showed me when a feeling was clearly formed from the lies of abuse or neglect, then how expel it. Or how to speak out the legitimate feelings and emotions in a nonconfrontational way without fear of rejection. It was a process of course.

My most sincere desire was to nurture and raise my child free from my residual struggles. With the knowledge I gained while being counselled, I was resolute in conquering the cycle of abuse! I would barrier myself off when I felt triggered by her just being a child. I was not going to lay a hand on her while I was emotionally unstable! Prayer was the avenue to the calm, the peace that surpassed all my understanding (Philippians 4:6-7). As I resisted, the hard hold over my emotions subsided (James 4:7:10).

When my daughter was about 4 years old, she was brushing my hair in the living room while I was seated on the floor. A rare escape from constantly having to play Barbies with her. She said that she wanted to get a different brush, so she ran off to the bathroom and came back with the item she had need of. A couple days went by, when I went for my only precious piece of jewelry, a necklace of diamond and gold. I couldn't find it anywhere. As I retraced my steps, I realized that I had placed it in the bathroom, on the back of the toilet

– where the brush had been that she collected earlier in the week. Instantly I knew what had happened, and it was long gone! I blew up at her, told her words that I wished I could have taken back that moment. But I was too enraged, to the point of dropping her off at her grandma's house for the day. I didn't even let my mom dissent.

It wasn't long after dropping her off that my mind shifted to God, and my words and actions toward my daughter. I had retaliated against an unknowing little child, unaware of what she had done. She was always so tender; she had asked me to stop acting out in her own little words. I still remember her pleading eyes, as I sat at the foot of my bed and told her I wanted to be away from her for a while. I would get over it, but I needed space. I felt it was the only way of doing it right, given my propensities. Then I repented, and the Lord soothed my soul once more. When I picked up my daughter, I only had patience and a purely generous heart for her. This was a new level of parenting and relating to her needs that I had stepped into. In words for her level of understanding, I also asked her to forgive me. This has lasted our whole life when we have argued or unrealistically expected something of each other.

Getting free from my suicidal angst took a few years, but it was all God once more! He first had to bring me through the process of letting go of strife and contentions stored up against others. Apparently, this added to my "what's the use in living" mentality. He put a picture in my mind's eye of me getting up on a "soapbox" and spewing my words of incrimination at my accusers and haters. Easily, I saw how it was me that needed forgiveness for the thoughts I was bringing against them. I was a sinner too. I formed a prayer for whenever I got up on my soapbox. It goes something like, "I forgive them, and I release them into your perfect will, my God." He also told me to pray, "The Lord is my Judge, my Jury and my Advocate. Then he told me to say out loud every day, "The Lord is my Helper, the Lord is my Keeper, the Lord is Provider". It's all there in the bible, I've found it all.

There was one more thing that needed to be brought out into the light for me to see that I was worthy of the life that he had given me. I was to see myself the way he sees me. It came about in a fantastic way, one morning in prayer. I was lingering, taking my time since it was a Saturday. I was thinking on his words from reading my bible, and then I would think about what it was I needed to do that day. Back and forth my mind rolled. While I was thinking about coloring my hair, which I did religiously for years, he started to intercept my thoughts. He told me that he had made me, impressing on me that nothing I could do would ever make me more precious than the way he had created me. I started to sooth myself, running my hands up and down my arms. He spoke how my body and hair color, my eyes, the way my intelligent mind works, all of it was his creation. I was an interpretation of his qualities and workmanship, a facet of his personality! My mind was blown over how he was relating me to him! Then he said that I was trying to legitimize myself, by the way I tried to change the way I looked. He said I was trying to bring attention to myself, but that he sees me, and loves me just the way I am.

Once again, his words brought overwhelming truth to the matter and I was convinced. I had indeed pursued attention getting tactics in the way I bleached the natural color from my hair. I was the darkest blonde in my family of towheads. To begin with, I wanted to be like them, but my melanin had always been a shade darker. This was most likely genetic traits of the Italian showing in me, whereas the Scandinavian was coming out in them. But it was one more thing I hated about myself that set me apart. It was easy to give into the Lord's loving words though, and so I let my hair color grow out.

I clearly remember as a kid, one day I finally noticed a big brown patch of skin on my right thigh. I yelled to my mom, there was something on my leg! She investigated it and laughed, saying it had been there my whole life. But why? She said it was probably melanin that hadn't distributed. She added that she really didn't know. Being young, I didn't understand at all. I just thought it made me look really weird. As I grew, I covered it up all the time. I didn't wear anything above my knees. The only exception was while in a swim suit. But as a Christian, I started wearing swim shorts for modesty, so even then it has been covered.

These little things about me influenced my self-hatred. As well as always being chided for "over think-ing" or "thinking too deep." The Lord straightened me out on all of it. Then he brought deliverance from sui-cide, self-hatred and depression. Once that was com-pleted, in a very diplomatic way, I would defend how I thought. I'd reply to any accuser a retort, that I liked the way my mind worked. How deep and vast and wide my thoughts could venture; it was the way I was created. This was the end of that incriminating tone, usually from my mom. I was becoming free from my past. She who the son has set free shall be free indeed! (John 8:31-36)

Poems:

-

Tear Jerk
Did you ever have a place
Where just because of grace
You could run a race
And actually finish in place?
I know I'm blessed, you see
Because that place is reality to me.

I've been given it for free
But it's the cost of life in me.

-

<u>*Untitled Poem*</u>
I chose to walk this way, I chose to die.
There hasn't been a moment that I regretted my reply.
Oh LORD, it's painful to stand alone,
It's so painful to hear my heart grown.
I'm young now, and my beauty is plain.
What will happen if I never know his name?
Today I can't help myself,
I feel empty inside.
I feel the pull of loneliness,
And it's only YOU who gets me by.
I have so much inside of me willing to share.
Let me share, LORD, let me share.
The days go by and roll away.
In my spirit I cry each day.
As if a crescendo builds, then fades away.
I want to share, I want to play!
Deliver, LORD, into that place
Where I no longer will get caught in the race.
But I will be in love, in life, in grace.
Forever with another face!

Chapter 5

My Mom and Me

I must have been about the same age as the hiding behind the couch incident when I first realized I didn't like my mom, because I knew she didn't like me much. On a summer day, I had been told to go lay down for a nap in her bed. She used to separate my sister and I for naps. I climbed in and was entertaining myself, which I did a lot. I would breathe through my mouth and use my throat to makes sounds. One was like a chain, as I breathed out slower the chain links clanked louder. I thought I was very talented at it! My mom came in to kiss me, a relatively benign habit for moms. But as she did, I stuck out my tongue. She startled back. That was the first time I resisted her kisses.

Years later, she would accuse me of not liking her, "even as a young child!" I countered, why was it my responsibility as a young child to make you feel liked?!

Weren't you the grown up, weren't you supposed to parent me? I was only feeding off your rejection of me, a young child!

These highly charged emotional confrontations never went well for me. My whole family had years to galvanize around my mom's emotional drama. I was always the bad guy for bringing up my baggage. None of my family wanted to know me, know what was going on inside of me. But this defense of hers that day, that I was responsible at a young age for her emotional well-being, made me realize that my mom was a narcissist. Then things started making a ton of sense.

One of my biggest questions growing up in that household was why did my mom stay with my step dad when he was clearly abusive to us. It seemed that my oldest sister was the only one immune, and as she got older, she played this card out to my detriment. We shared a room most of our childhood, so if I made her mad, she would scream, "Dad, Leslie's doing ...!" Next thing that happened would be him opening the door and me getting clobbered. He would go out and she would snicker while I cried. He was meanest to my brother, as I stated before. But many times, my brother and I would try to hide from him together. I remember the basement of the house we lived in when they got married. It had shelves with sliding doors across them. We would climb in those and close the doors. In the last house we all lived in, my dad had built shelves downstairs. We would climb them up to the top and hide from him. But those were open shelves, so dad would find us and pull us down as we cried out. I'm as sympathetic to memories regarding my brother as I am my own.

As an adult, my mom told me that she and my older sister went to a woman's house and knocked on the door, asking for my step dad. The woman came to the door, then closed it. My step dad opened it next. He was indeed with another woman. My mom simply asked him to come home or she was taking us and leaving, so he came home. I can't imagine why my mom put up with it. She was also verbally abused by him too.

All the things that happened, to me, my siblings and my mom were horrible, but my dad could also be endearing. I have memories of his good moods and our drives, our camping trips, our holidays with his large family. I remember his defense of me when my mom would complain to him about me.

I remember at ten, I was vacuuming and not liking it, so I was muttering. My mom came over and pulled the vacuum cord out of the socket. Angrily, she literally seethed out, "Do you know that I asked your dad who he favored, and he said you?! He said of all my kids, he thought you would be the one to make it, because you're smart!" She hated that, because she favored my older sister, actually admired her. That day she told me to shut up and just do my job!

I was about the same age when we went on a drive to my aunt and uncle's house. The adults sat in the kitchen and chatted while we kids were expected to entertain ourselves. My sister asked to listen to music. She put "Tapestry" by Carole King on the record player. I fell in love with that album! But I got bored so I crept around the corner of the kitchen, waiting to see if there was any sign that we'd be leaving soon. That's when I heard my mom start berating me to my aunt and uncle. She ended by calling me fat, to which my dad said, "She's not fat, she's just pleasingly plump" to which he got a good laugh all around. I was devastated!

I knew that my mom treated me different. This became more of a tribal distinction as I got older, and more overweight. No surprise that I was eating my emotions. I was not allowed into the fridge like my siblings though. If they went in the fridge for a snack, I was told by my mom to eat something different than them. This seemed to galvanize a them versus me dynamic. It was pretty obvious that the pups were going the way of the mother. It hardened me considerably.

I didn't have any friends either. My mom thought I did, but the block was full of friends that would seemingly let me play with them, but would eventually call me names and make fun of my fatness. I was one hundred fifty pounds at ten years old. I remember sitting on the outside steps alone most of the time with a Barbie or something else to pass the time. This is when

I started to feel a loneliness inside that took years to overcome.

On days when I couldn't handle the drama inside the house, I would go out to the garage and cut my wrists. I'd go in there and find a razor off dad's workbench and try to cut deep enough to hit a vein. I'd "practice" up and down my arm. I am amazed that nobody ever seemed to notice the cuts. This was after houses had been built up around us and no more fields were available to go sit in and watch the fire burn with my matches. I'd turn over and over in my mind what I'd like to do to the members of my family inside that house. Those thoughts were usually interrupted by the blood on my arms and the pain I was inflicting on myself, enough pain for each time I tried.

It was at this same time that my school was offering instruments to use, practice and then play, as part of a training program for future marching band placements. I was in elementary school and I wanted a French horn so bad! The school had only two, and I applied for one. I was not accepted, which seemed to finish the deteriorating of my esteem. I was good at so many things, like spelling and math, but I couldn't see it because my esteem was crushed. Later in a higher grade level art class, I drew a French horn in black charcoal that was really well done. I guess that French horn dream died hard.

At home, I was becoming more rebellious. I had started to snoop through other people's stuff. I guess in my immature mind I was thinking that if they weren't going to open up to me, I would snoop through and find stuff myself. Wrong idea, because I found a crucial item, that would cause me no further forward movement. At a time when a child needs to be nurtured, to find and explore new ideas and concepts, pushed toward aspirations, I was devastated in my tracks because I found a suicide note that my mom had written. It was slid under other papers, in an envelope of its own, in her dresser drawer. My world stood still. I stopped breathing, then one breath, then another. I had to do something but I was in no position to do anything. I had nobody to bring this to and I had found it while snooping! It was one thing to find Christmas presents that you actually wanted, only to see them go to my sister when wrapped. It was another to bring this proposed deed to anyone since it had been hidden to begin with.

I put it away, and I started to watch my mom for signs that she would carry out this deed! I always came home right after school, but it was now paramount to do so – forget any offer to play an instrument! I was on watch duty. I can remember during that time, one day coming home to find my mom napping. You know what I was thinking! So, I woke her up and she was mad. I did enough strange stuff during that time to finally solicit curiosity from my mom. I admitted to her what I had found. She didn't reassure me in the least bit, she just said it was a bad day, and that's it. Then she gave me a very cold shoulder, making me feel her wrath for doing something wrong. I guess this was a clue to her narcissism. The feeling of being the guilty one plagued me for most of my life until I resisted it.

When I was thirteen, I remember my mom doing something for me that I will never forget though. I alluded to this before, but will again because it was a pivot from the chaos and dark mentality that I lived in. On my birthday, my mom got me a brown crossbody purse and inside was a small note pad and a pencil. That day she gave to me two gifts; she had listened, plus she got me something regarding what I had talked about, being a writer. She told me to take notes when I was inspired, because that's what writers do.

One of my mom's narcissistic tendencies was to weigh herself every single day, until she couldn't walk on her own anymore. When my weight loss came, during the summer that I was raped, I got respect for it from her. She seemed to think that attention from men was very important. Keeping one's weight down was crucial. Even as an elderly woman, she was always looking around to see if any men were checking her out. Suffice to say, this was the environment I grew up in, so I began seeking male attention too.

My folks' house was the first to be built on our block and as houses went up around us, more kids my age started moving in. I hung out with a couple of girls that lived on the opposite side of the block, outside of my mom's line of sight. These girls were a couple years older, but it didn't matter because we were all looking for attention. The houses on that side of the block were low-income homes. My friends' moms were single, and one was not home much due to work. The other girl became my best friend over the years. Her mom was home because she ran a daycare. At the house with no supervision, we had plenty of time to test out pot and listen to new music. I even got my ears pierced there, using an ice cube and sewing needle. I don't recommend it!

I was becoming a flirt, which evolved into vanity. Vanity is a very real, dark entity and very deceptive. I can recall how I was transformed by the use of make-up. Once I had it on, I became a different type of character. I began play acting this pretty creature that could flirt with men easily. As I got older, this became more precisely defined and effortless. I was a pretty young woman, even without the theatrics. But I didn't know it, I needed the demon to help me come out. And this is how it got it's hooks in me.

Once vanity was established, I was fair game for promiscuity. And my best friend was just as curious as me. Since my home life sucked, I would stay overnight at her house a lot on weekends. As we hung out, our moms met and became friends too. Weekend sleepovers evolved into whenever we had something planned. We would slip out of her bedroom window and meet up with guys to drive around and get high. Then we would sneak back in the window unnoticed.

There was a roller rink up the block from where we lived. We had a ton of fun there meeting guys, going home on time, then sneaking out to finish the night. But when her mom started living with a boyfriend, we got busted. I don't really remember that slowing us down much though. One morning, after we stayed out all night long, we came walking in the front door of my best friend's house. We were going to get cleaned up and still go to school, since this was a weekday. When we walked into the split-level entrance, I could hear her mom say to my mom over the phone not to worry, that the girls will turn up soon. Then she saw us and she shouted into the phone, "The QUEENS are home!" We listened to the lectures and went to school. Nothing changed.

I had another friend that I was very close to, who lived right across the street from the high school. She had two older brothers, one a motorhead and one just a "head." The head was the source for the best weed. My friend also had two younger sisters, both gorgeous girls. They were like little sisters to me. I had many good and bad times with all the siblings of this family. The motorhead ended up losing his life at a very young age to the stoned husband of one of his younger sisters. The other beautiful sister was thrown from a truck that her husband was driving. He was racing down a county road when he hit a culvert. She flew out the windshield and landed face first on the pavement. Her face was smashed and rebuilt. After many surgeries he was still pretty, though scarred.

On weekends I'd sleep over at this friend's house too. At night we ran the streets with her brothers, getting into whatever trouble was out there. I loved when the motorhead finished a car, because we'd all pile in and go to the Sun Drive-In, down in the city. It was hot for dope and racing down there! I met guys, but it was always a bit riskier to go out with them. I would end up staying out way too late coming and going. It didn't matter, I'd take the heat. They seemed to be much more mature and definitely cuter that the guys from my area.

I had been hit and grounded for running wild, but nothing was working to tone me down. My mom took a stand down position as I grew older. She was hesitant to tell my dad anymore for fear he would hurt me too badly. She started letting me out when I shouldn't have been allowed, like when she was called by the police department because I had been caught shop lifting. That day, my friend and I had decided to go lift an outfit to wear for the party her brothers were having that night. When we were caught, her father came to get us from the police station. He was in a very agitated and disappointed mood. He dropped me off at my house. Once inside, I pleaded with my mom to still let me go to the party, and she did.

I was a strong debater in high school, so in English class when classmates didn't want to work, they asked me to start a debate with the teacher. I was happy to, but this got old when really, I just didn't want to be there. Sometimes I would walk out mid-session, right under the arm of the teacher trying to ban the doorway. Skipping was normal now and getting high with the same type of people during a school day was "cool." Sometimes I'd spend afternoons high and learning about sex with a cute guy.

With all the skipping and truancy, I was sent to court by the school. I was deemed "Incorrigible" by the court and placed on strict in-school perimeters. But that did not change my home life drama. As I came and went, it became clear to my mom that I was not going to listen and she signed papers of custody over to the woman I babysat for up the block.

From time to time, I would get involved with very nice men, and I would bring them home for my mom's approval. Sometimes she cared, and other times she would just rub my nose in the fact that I couldn't keep a man, so why would this one be different. I never stopped caring what she thought. But I wouldn't listen to her either because I was so jaded. Like her insistence to dump the abusive guy. I would go see my mom with black eyes and bruises when I was with him. For the most part, she would stay silent, she knew that it would go in one ear and out the other.

When I miscarried the abusive guy's baby, she was glad and offered no sympathy. When I had my daughter, she was there to go through the pregnancy with me. After the baby was born though, she made it clear that she was not open to babysitting. The loneliness was acute at times, but it made me grow. My baby grew into a child and I grew into a reasonably responsible adult.

My family was not there for most of it. I remember being on WIC while my daughter was an infant and one day my car was stolen. When I went out to load my baby into the car seat to go get to our WIC appointment, there was no car! I was stunned! I went back in and started calling anyone I could think of to take me to that appointment because I needed the food. I called my sister, but she was "packing for their annual Hawaii trip" and couldn't be bothered. I finally found an aunt to take me. Those years, when my daughter was a baby, were very hard for me to get by.

Then I became a Christian, and my thoughts and prayers were about doing right for my daughter and myself. I started molding myself after ladies in the church, and when I had an issue formed out of past experiences, I would take it to trusted church friends for counsel and prayer. I broke the cycles of abuse and promiscuity, becoming free through deliverance. It was not easy, many times I would lock myself away so I would not act out when I felt triggered. I leaned into the Lord, understanding more and more that those were the times to go to him, and stop running in shame from him.

Then I made the decision to leave my chosen profession for the sake of my daughter. I describe it as walking off a diving board backwards. I didn't know what I was going to do, but by then I had experienced healings and knew that I could trust God. I was making this decision for our good. I knew that he, being a loving father to her, could be trusted to make a way where there seemed to be no way.

As one job led to another, I gained comprehensive knowledge and a better wage. I didn't mind that my family didn't approve, calling it job hopping. I was gaining a living wage and more experience to obtain better positions. I was long past thinking that our society remains loyal to a company for years until retirement. I had met those that were forced into retirement or the company had laid them off. I had a "do for myself" attitude, while always praying for right positions. Eventually it became somewhat of a testimony, because I always got a job with no long wait in between.

I attest that this was because of his first word to me, "Tithe." I have been faithful to do it ever since!

My life progressively got fuller with church functions for adult and child. As my faith grew, my mom would listen, but she was unwilling to accept information regarding faith from me. Eventually she said it was because I was such a yo-yo. It was true, I still had weaknesses especially where men were concerned. But as my faith deepened, she became more open. She made the choice to step away from Catholicism and joined a bible study for women, hosted at a Lutheran church. She went every week for years and grew in bible knowledge. She loved the teacher and the group so much! It was really a wonderful thing to see her grasping bible truths.

My relationship with my mom improved, but we still had our times of dissention. I was always the last to get her attention, even if I called her long distance. She often said to me, "Listen, can I call you back?" I'd wait, especially if I had something to tell her about my daughter. But that call back wouldn't come. After a week or so I was the person to eventually dial the phone again.

One year on Mother's Day, I decided to write a poem for my mom. I used a pretty font, and printed it on good paper stock. I presented it to her as if it were a gift. She read it, and I earnestly waited for her pleasurable comments. However, her reaction to it was a disdain for the words that I so carefully chose to draw a picture on the page. I was completely deflated, asking her what I could ever do to have any semblance of regard from her? She said in an unemotional way, that she didn't agree with what I wrote about her. I didn't try to explain, I really didn't have it in me to try.

-

Poem:

For You
In my mind's eye there is a place where you exist, by your presence and influence in my life.

This is the place I would like to tell you about. I may be driving down the road and think of you. What my mind and heart captures of that thought, is the place where you exist.

The place is warm, a bright yellow summer day. The day is yellow, not blue. I think because of how warm your existence is there. I see you seated at peace, in quiet contemplation. Very much like how you sit on your chair at the desk. In my mind's eye I don't know what it is you are thinking about. But, as I describe it to you, I can tell you are probably thinking about one of your kids, maybe me.

There is no room for strife, just peace there in that place you share in my mind's eye. The grace is full around you, as if the very air where you are seated is grace. Maybe grace is the color yellow, which I painted for the warmth in that place you exist. The peace and the quiet reflection on your face is how I've painted the objective, positive influence you've had in my life.

I don't see you as young, you are pictured in my mind's eye as you are now. The creases in your face I've let exist there for the wisdom you've shared with me over the years. I haven't set you apart, a picture of the realism of life which you have taught me.

There is another person who shares this place with you in my mind's eye. HE is responsible for creating the place you exist. For without HIS love and grace in both our lives, I could never describe this place. I would not know what grace looks like. Certainly, I would not know how to paint such a loving picture where you exist in my mind's eye.

To be fair, as I reread this, the last line strikes me as a bit insensitive and I'm sorry for that. I had the best intentions when I wrote this for her. I was trying to express the love of God for both of us and what it had done for our relationship in me. I guess my truth transparently slipped in. Needless to say, I just wanted her approval.

Toward the later years of her life, we were bonded over our shared faith in Christ. Then one day, about six years before she left this earth, she called me to express her sincere apology. She said that she was reading the bible and saw how Jacob had favored Joseph, and what this favoring in the family did to his brothers. (Genesis 37:3-4) She said she felt the Lord touch her with sorrow for all the years she showed favor to everyone, especially her youngest, over me. She could see the damage it had caused. I slumped down next to my bed, in my bedroom where I had taken her call. I remember we spoke very softly now, understanding flowed through the phone line. Below is what I wrote in a journal regarding this experience.

Journal Entry:

It's the week of Thanksgiving, my favorite holiday! GOD has manifested a wonderful, renewed relationship with my mom. She has said more to me this year to bolster and say her praise of me as her daughter. She has been touched and changed by GOD, voicing her repentant heart to me regarding our relationship. She asked forgiveness for favoritism of my siblings over me, and what it must have done to me. To that one thing, I replied that if I never heard another word from her, that would be enough! It covered over my entire life of hurt and aggravation from her and toward her. Since our conversation, we have been more like friends. Though we are still us, we are hearing each other. I am deeply grateful for what GOD has done for us! I am so thankful!!

The day my mom died I was not able to be at her side. My sisters and their daughters who were, called my daughter and I and placed us on speaker phone. We all offered our words and expressed our love to our mom and grandmom. She was no longer conscious, though we made references to different breathing patterns as proof that she might still hear us. This was day four of a brain bleed that she had suffered while in the hospital. She was awaiting a bed to open in hospice because she was "sundowning," a word I learned then. The day of the brain bleed, she closed her eyes and had not opened them since. She was transferred home on this fourth day of her DNR, her last day with no water.

I didn't want to be there to see her state anyway. I had been to see her in the hospital while she was still conscious. Even prior to that, we had experienced a couple days where my mom and I spoke to each other of our truth, our love and she was ready. During the last chance I had, before she was admitted to the hospital, she and I took a ride on a warm winter day. That day I parked at the local lake and we talked, rather, she talked and I listened. My mom was happiest to be listened to. She talked of her childhood mostly. I had no idea then, that this was part of the sundowning process. As we sat in my truck, when we were facing each other, I said to her that I loved her. She replied that she loved me too, and she hadn't, but that was water under the bridge.

By her saying that, I had years and years of emotions, feelings of worthlessness, clashes, unwelcomed devotion, all confirmed! I was vindicated – it was never just in my head! She just admitted that she had not loved me. But then and there, with a split second to revel, I was completely in tune with my mom... my mom and me were good!

Now she was going home. She knew Christ as her Savior, indeed I had no struggle seeing her off. Just the pain of all those years and wanting a redo. But she and I had come to a loving end and I loved her so much!

As we were huddled, I sang her two worship songs over the phone. Then I perceived and said these words, "I think mom is like a dog, trying to be on her best behavior for us all." I was not at all calling my mom a dog, just pointing out behavior. Her breathing would get stronger in response to us speaking to her, as it did while I sang. We agreed and decided to take a breather and reconvene on the phone in twenty minutes.

When we came back together, she did indeed breath her last. I asked my sister to bring the phone to her mouth so I could make sure that she wasn't still there. My sister confirmed she was gone, and they used a stethoscope to hear no heartbeat. We were called together for her passing and it was done. But hanging up didn't seem correct. I asked if they were sure she was gone? My sister later recalled that my question was so sad to hear, as I struggled to process that she was no longer alive.

It was such a deeply personal emotion I was feeling. For someone who doesn't like funerals, this was making it very clear why I don't: I had to process it by myself. I knew my daughter had a close relationship with her grandma so I knew she was very emotional too. We stayed on the phone briefly after the others hung up. We knew, though, that there were no more words that could be shared at that moment, just pain in our hearts. After I hung up, I slept a bit, then wept most the night. By the next morning, I needed an outlet for my feelings so I wrote a song to her, my mom.

Song:

-

Say It Now
Bridge
I, I'm losing you
Wedding clothes look good on you
Think I'm gonna wear them too
I, I'm losing you
Wedding clothes look good on you
Think I'm gonna wear them too
Didn't want our time to end
But you were always with your friends
Even though it wasn't me

Did some time to get relief
All those days all those ways
When it comes down
Grace by grace turns time around
Bridge
Cheated then but look at now
We know what they don't know how
We all grow tall we all get small
Punctuation on the crowd
Your freedom gives my eye free reign
Precious is your departing frame
An endless love is what we'll gain!
End
I'm losing you!
Those wedding clothes look good on you!
Capture me in your rear view!
Place your heart is what I'll do.
I love, I love you!

We lost her and my step dad within a five-month period of each other. It was the timeframe that caused the most shock and grief to our systems. I am completely at peace with my memories now and I know they are in God's Kingdom. Jesus spoke to me to give him my heart in the earliest days of my salvation. He promised me then that my whole family would be saved. All is good, and I'm sure she is proud of me.

Chapter 6

Underpinnings of a Glorious Relationship

After I was filled with the Spirit there were rough times, but eventually things improved. I mentioned prior that my step dad called my church a cult. He got crueler; he said if it was a "real" church then I wouldn't be such a bitch. Then the rest of my family banded together with that same chant.

This banding together started earlier though because smart children sense their atmosphere. When my mom clearly had no time for me, my siblings followed suit. After I joined the church, I became devastatingly lonely. It was hard to start friendships with the close-knit members of the church, and now my family was backing away from me even more.

That first church was a suburban church and the families that went there for a long time were very close. Some lived on the same streets. I found it very painful to go there on Sundays and go home after church with nothing more to look forward to until Wednesday evening. I was starved for fellowship, but I also felt different, from my clothes to my kid. I cut off my hair into a short, tailored style and started dressing more conservatively. I couldn't do anything about my over active three-year-old! The rest of those kids seemed very docile and tame.

I remember going home one Sunday and climbing into my bed with my daughter to read, hoping we could take a nap. She took the book from me and was fake reading to me. All at once I started crying from sheer loneliness, I couldn't hold it in. I got so loud my daughter thought I was laughing! Her misunderstanding made me laugh and I quit crying. I praised God for her!

I made horrendous mistakes in the church early on too, because I didn't know any better. I wanted to be a missionary so I applied to Youth With a Mission (YWAM) New Zealand, which at the time was the only family camp they offered for missions training. After making application, I received a letter that I had been accepted and a portion of the funds would be due by a certain date. I was beginning to learn about faith, only just enough to wrongly apply it in this situation. I didn't tell anyone about the need for my tuition, I just believed the money would come. I wasn't being secretive; I was doing things the way I always had, with no input or supervision as it concerned me.

When the money did not come in, I received a call from the school. I apologized that I didn't have the funds, so I wasn't able to come. The person on the other end of the call was very formal and expressed what the normal process would have looked like, asking me if I understood. Possibly they thought I might attempt the enrollment again. I was very downcast about the whole thing. However, the YWAM base called the pastor listed on my application too. Next, I received the only call I ever got from the pastor. He explained that he had been informed of my application to join and that I had held open the position in a promise to pay. He said the base explained that there were other families that were waitlisted and could have applied had I called them sooner to withdraw. Then he asked why I had not come to him for counsel and prayer about it? I was stunned by this question. I replied that I guess I didn't know I had to. I'm not sure he understood my answer from my point of view though. I did not have a family structure that taught me to seek out counsel. It was a mistake I never made again.

I got into a church cell group with a missionary emphasis and started taking short-term trips that were arranged through my church instead. As I look back, God's hand was in those details. Shortly after that, he gave me the "big picture." I was to stay state-side and raise my daughter with a presence of mind, so that my impact would be greater on her life.

After several years at the suburban church, I felt the Lord speak to me that he wanted me to go and see what the rest of his body was doing. I was kind of comfortable in my lonely but stable existence, so it was like peeling my hands off the steering wheel to let him drive. I found out later they call that "white knuckle ministry", when the Lord beckons you and you submit even though you don't want to because of fear. In my case it was mostly fear of the unknown. I've had many experiences like that, when I've been afraid to "let go and let God!"

I met some really wonderful people at my first church too. I had a beautiful friend whom I kind of idolized. It turned out we had a similar background in regards to drug usage, but she was married with two beautiful kids by the time I met her. We did as much as we could together, but the restraints of a single gal trying to plan things with a married gal left me wanting more. I had another friend that was a teacher, and on weekends she was a stealth evangelist! She had so many hook ups in the city that I loved going with her to see where we could minister.

I had an exciting experience in a bar with my teacher friend one time. Yeah, I was back in the trenches, but this time it was totally different. We would stand around until we were led to start a conversation with an individual, or someone would start up one with us. I got good at feeling out exactly how I could engage at a level of mutual experience, then I would wind it around to their need for a Savior and how I had found him.

My teacher friend and I got so comfortable evangelizing together that we would use vacation time to go to large cities and have spiritual "scavenger hunts." We would pray and let God lead us to where we could have the most impact. Those were awesome trips! We saw salvations in the worst places. We would get words for huge institutions and brazenly walk around the grounds praying or doing weird stuff like praise with tambourines. It was truly freeing, but crazy to the natural eye. We were just learning obedience to do whatever we felt the Holy Spirit leading us to do. Sometimes my daughter was with us, or my mom would reluctantly watch her if she wasn't too busy. Her reluctancy was only toward me, because she loved her grandchild.

While I was still at the suburban church, I had my first encounter with a prophetic word spoken over me. This is that word:

"For the strength of My will is on thee and thou shall not waiver. But you're loosed in the glory and you're healed by the strength and the glory and the stripes of thy God. Walk in the favor of it, loose the song of the Lord. Loose the vision of our God. For I have healed and strengthened you. I've forgiven, you forget it. Let your emotions and let that which try to depress – I've cut it from you. And you shall be yea, strong in Me!

Stir up the gift, move in the glory of thy God. Begin to speak in the prophetic anointing, for the Lord will raise up many. As you speak My word, My touch is upon you, and the humbleness and contriteness of our God shall bring it to pass. Now, that which you've been robbed of for the last six years, I'm going to restore. I'm going to bring you the desire of your heart. Your heritage shall not be limited, for you will be blessed financially and I'll promote you. And your family shall rejoice! Amen!"

I was becoming aware that my intuitive nature may well be from my spiritual gifts. Sometimes I would be able to read a room and know what people were going to do or say next. I was always aware that my mind worked in vivid, colorful pictures, that it was my way of intellectualizing the world around me. I had a huge imagination and dreamed every night in color. Also, I am able to hear high and low pitch resonance sound waves that others can't hear.

Once, I dreamt of a house I had lived in as a renter. The house had a dried-up pool in the backyard while I was renting it. I dreamt the pool had been covered over. Since that house was nowhere near where I was now living, it was not something that I would know. However, a long time after the dream, I went down the road that house was on and saw through the trees that there was no more pool. This is one example of how the gift was operating prior to my salvation. I honestly believe people are born with their spiritual gifts.

Now that I was filled with the Spirit, this was coming out in my mind's eye in positive affirmations. First, I saw a banner over my apartment door that read, "I know nothing and it's okay." God was forming a threshold of peace within me. Next, I saw "His Banner Over Me is Love!" over the doorway of our dining room in the first house I bought. (Song of Solomon 2:4)

The prophetic nature of my gift was starting to take shape too. I would get words from the Lord about issues people were dealing with, which seemed to encourage them when I shared. I'd get words of prophecy regarding our nation too, but nobody wanted to hear those because I was a nobody.

I also started to see the same type of corporate ladder in the church that I had seen in the professional world. In the church there seemed to be a glass ceiling for females just like in the working world. Regardless of whether they thought that I hadn't been a Christian long enough, I was a single mother. It was a time when these issues were weighted against me.

I followed the leading of the Lord and went on my way to an inner-city church. I met a very outgoing woman right away. She had a small business, cleaning repossessed properties. She hired me to help, since I had given up my chosen profession to be more present for my daughter.

My profession would cause me to work late and on weekends. Sometimes my child would fall asleep in class because she wasn't getting picked up on school nights from the various sitters I could find until quite late. By the time I quit my job, I had exhausted all sitting options and I had to latch key her at the age of six! So, I started cleaning and painting these repossessed houses.

While working, we would listen to a bible teacher on the radio, but we couldn't figure out if it was a man or a woman. We came to find out it was Joyce Meyer, back when Joyce was on radio only. The hours of teaching I absorbed in those days was priceless for someone as broken as I was. I clearly remember being coached by the voice of Joyce Meyer to "do it afraid!" I bought books and tapes from Joyce's ministry and handed those down to others when I was finished with them. My daughter was listening too, on weekends in my own home. I also remember going to one of Joyce's live ministry events. I was being built up from the ground up!

The inner-city church is also where I really got into short-term, inner-city missions. As a group, we went to New York, San Francisco, Los Angeles, along with our own city streets. My daughter was thriving in that church and would be out on the streets ministering with me at home. She was only six and getting a taste for ministry. She led our neighbor's six-year-old son to the Lord while riding bikes with him one day. She hit the brakes on her bike and looked straight at him saying, "Brent, do you want to follow Jesus?" He said yes to that and she told him how to pray. She told me afterward, in a very confident, but excited voice!

I was pretty fearless about my faith too. I compared myself with the statement King David made in response to his wife, when she told him he looked like a fool dancing before the Ark. He said that he would dance, sing and worship God with abandon, even if it made him look undignified! (2 Samuel 6:12-23) I had finally found a cause, the truth, and I was a warrior inside!

After a couple years, being led by the Holy Spirit, I went on to another inner-city church. This church had a very ambitious pastor that took on a lot of projects benefiting both the members and the people of the surrounding area. There was a lunch after every Sunday service that would feed the church goers and the neighborhood, and a free housing advocacy meeting held after the lunch. When the pastor met me and I shared some of my evangelistic zeal, he put me in charge of the housing meeting. He said he needed a bright person to take initiative with difficult issues like unlawful detainers. I had some property management knowledge, so I said yes. Sundays became a long day of service and fun!

It was there that I met a large family with such a generous spirit, all eight of them actively serving in the church kitchen! In time, the mom and I became good friends, while my daughter was best friends with one her girls. A pastor friend of theirs had come to the church for lunch one Sunday, so I was introduced to him. As I got to know him, he greatly added to my view of the church.

He had been trained in bible college and been affiliated with a well-known denomination. But he became disillusioned with the church structure resembling a corporation, which I could fully understand. His idea of the body coming together for church at the local level included input from everyone as the Spirit guided. He was always right there to temper or correct if someone got off the rails, but that was how the church learned. He also taught we can give at least a tithe, to be used to free up people for ministry and helping people in need. But building costs should come out of additional offerings meant to support those expenses. He did not have his own church building. His meetings were always housed in a church, whether a rented basement or a parish he timeshared and used on Saturday.

This intrigued me so much; it was where my daughter and I went next, following our big family friends. It was in this kind of setting that my gifts were able to be used and sharpened. I grew tremendously under his ministry. He showed me one of the best examples I've had of a true, modern-day disciple.

Our ambitious pastor of the inner-city church had left without much notice, which is why we left. Another church had bought the property but we were not availed the same functionary positions. We were not even sure the church wouldn't just be sold again, for the purpose of tearing it down. There wasn't a lot of assurances being offered. A woman pastor was heading up the transition team for the church that purchased the property. While at a meeting where she had called us all together, she prayed over us, asking God to lead her in blessing us. As she prayed over me, she spoke this prophetic word: "*You see what the Lord sees!*"

These prophetic words spoken over me were able to be put into operation under this new pastor in a supervised setting. It was extraordinary as we, the members, were able to minister and see people saved and delivered! Others heard by word of mouth and came to our meetings to get free from demons and spiritual bondages. We had lots of anointing with great successes! This pastor was very hands on and offered one on one training in the ministry, which I accepted. I was licensed the following year.

Through my initial journey in and out of several churches, I had seen that each church was established in different strengths and emphasis. They were living and vibrant, much like individual beings. I had witnessed churches that reach out far to find those in need, and churches that reach closer to home, using missionaries to do the farthest reaching. There were big congregations and smaller ones. I was personally in favor of the small, more intimate settings where iron could sharpen iron. It was what I needed to continue my growth in freedom and faith.

I also witnessed many miracles happen in the church, and on the streets as well. Once during a short-term inner city mission trip to Los Angeles, on Santa Monica boulevard I met a trans sex worker and we started talking. He was really tall and I kept having to look up. I asked if I could buy him a coffee, so we could sit down. He reluctantly said yes and followed me into a little kiosk type coffee shop not far from where he had been working the street corner. I had a very down to earth conversation with him about the type of life he was living, getting to the point of asking if he wanted to pray for his salvation. He said yes, so we reached our hands across the table to hold as we prayed. Then the power of God came right into that tiny coffee shop and fell on him. He sat there and quaked under the power, while I watched not saying a word! When he opened his eyes, I simply said, "God is real, isn't he?" To which he nodded his head up and down, tears running down his face. I gave him a napkin and asked if he was going to continue to do what he was doing, selling himself. He answered very honestly that he didn't know because it's how he paid the bills. I said that was a fair answer before we drifted back outside. Right then one of the other street ministers was looking for me, so I said goodbye and left him on that street. I knew in my heart that God had him now and all would work out for him. I never worried about my own safety, and always heeded the directions of our leaders. But my loyalty was to God. If he said go here or do that, I'd do it. I always saw the best responses that way.

It was on one of those ministry trips in San Francisco when the Lord called me to California. He spoke to me clearly as I stood against a fence, on an overcast, chilly day. He said, "Would you come here for me?" I instantly said, "No, Lord! What about my daughter?!" He responded to that by asking me to trust him with her. I immediately started telling my group what I heard, wondering out loud if he would ask me to bring my young child to such a place? The city that I knew was the underbelly, where sex, drugs and the throwaways lived. It was hard coming on these trips to any large city and see people – people made by God for a purpose, living under such demonic influences. Their response was overwhelmingly yes, if God had asked, he could provide. But I left for home not convinced that it was safe for her. I was fearless about the streets, but I feared when it came to my daughter. Besides, I loved my home state then and wasn't interested in leaving. He was asking me to bring her out to a state that I had no prior thoughts of moving to.

Back home when I told my mom she immediately shook her head no! I was still so emotionally tied to her apron strings for any involvement I could get, that I allowed her fear for our safety to dominate. I kept going on the short-term trips though. When I was back in San Francisco, inside a church waiting for our Sunday service to begin, the Lord spoke to me. He said that I feared man more than the reverential fear he asked of me. He said that he would have to put me back in the oven. Yep, I knew what he meant; it was a reference to burning off the dross in heating metals. Only the purest form comes out. He wanted all my devotion. I sat soberminded at this. It started stirring things up in me about the prospect of going out there for him.

From the point of giving my heart to Jesus and cultivating the presence of God in my life, I had been freed from demonic oppression, suicidal thoughts and tendencies, split personality disorder, loss of self-esteem, healing of heart issues, liver issues, nerve issues, and the list goes on. It took time and it was a progression. That's why I love these verses, "precept upon precept and line upon line," (Is 28:13) "from grace upon grace," (John 1:16 NASB) and "glory to glory"! (2 Cor 3:18) The book of Romans, Chapter 8 is a favorite of mine too, because the whole chapter speaks about the new life in Christ, how nothing can be stripped away from us that has been attained through his sufferings for us. Also, what we may go through can't compare to what he has for us! I'll take those words to the bank any day. Look up these verses and see for yourself; his promises are for you and cannot be revoked, unless you walk away from him.

Because of my freedom from demonic strongholds, I gained an early understanding of the supernatural. I used to reach out my arms and say I was touching the unseen world of sprits. I actually view life as an inter-action with the unseen realm as we go about our days. I have gotten to the point of seeing our world as the temporary, natural place my physical body exists, but it's not the one I am focused on. Just as the prophet spoke to his servant that there was indeed more with them, though not seen, I consciously make the choice to understand the unseen realm and view it just as real as where I'm sitting. (2 Kings 6:17-20) I see from God's Word that angels can help at my discretion, for my sustenance and sovereignty here on this side. Every-thing that I go through is another way of casting my existence on God. Every experience is to gain greater dependency on him, creating greater faith in me.

The fear of the Lord is the beginning of wisdom, and knowledge of the holy one is understanding. (Proverbs 9:10) That night, when he revealed his power and might, but also how he would take care of me when he spoke the word "Tithe", I understood to take him at his word. It began with an intense interest to study the bible. One way I got the written word into me was to read a Proverb for each day of the calendar month. I did this every day for about two years. I still go back to that pattern if I find I'm not remembering certain verses. His word is living water and we must drink it for the benefits of it. I also speak into my atmosphere or domain with the written word, letting all beings know, seen and unseen, that his word is my highest order. My home is my holy place where I commune with God. No demons are allowed in my territory!

Chapter 7

The Ride Begins

I was not doing well financially in the early days of my Christianity. I wasn't in debt, but I earned just enough for our living expenses. My car gave out one Sunday while we were at the small church. I went out to the parking lot to leave but we weren't going anywhere. The car's front end had rusted through and the body of the car was sitting on the tires. It could have been a disaster had it happened on the freeway! I praised God that it didn't, knowing he had protected us! I had to find a church option closer to home though. I didn't know how long it would be until I had a car again. I decided to try a church that I had heard was moving in some of the same anointing as the Brownsville revival.

Once I got established at the new church closer to home, I started participating in a healing ministry that took place there. I completed a group training with the leader, who was a powerful woman of God. I attended the healing ministry on a regular basis to pray for people. We would start with intercessory prayer in the back room of the church, while our leader would teach a short bible lesson in the sanctuary on healing for the people who had come for prayer. "Healing is the children's bread!" I heard her say so many times from the sanctuary.

During this time my younger sister had a baby boy. The first time I held him I knew there was something wrong with his eyes. I only mentioned it once, but my sister took him to the doctor to be examined. The doctor confirmed that the baby could barely see because his corneas were convex, instead of concave. They would require surgery.

I went to the healing ministry that week with a throbbing burden to pray for my new nephew's eyes. While we were praying in back, I asked my partners if we could pray for my nephew. As we did, my prayer in tongues morphed into a high-pitched octave note, which I held in a long breath. As I rather sang this out, I heard our leader in the sanctuary say to her audience, "My, I think we've got angels praying back there today!" It's the first time this happened to me, but I've experienced similar intercession since. That day I wasn't deterred; I didn't stop until I had a peace within that my nephew had been healed. He was, completely!

No treatment was ever needed, and still today there is nothing wrong with his eyes.

During my involvement with the healing ministry, I began to experience excruciating lower back pain when I made certain movements. It started to affect my right leg with numbness and before I knew it, I was dragging my leg because I had no feeling left. I went to a doctor and it was confirmed that there was at least one severely bulging disc in my spine which pressed on nerves causing the numbness in my leg. The doctor went on to tell me my options for treatment, and it was at that moment when I experienced what I can only describe as an out of body experience. While he was talking, I wasn't hearing his voice anymore, though I saw his lips moving. I saw myself get up and walk out of the clinic to the parking lot where I got in my car and drove away. Then I was back. I politely thanked him and left without committing to further treatment.

I knew as soon as I had this experience what it meant and what I was being asked to do. I was not going to be involved with a medical fix to this problem. I was to exercise my faith; this was a call. I went back to the church and asked for prayer from my healing room partners. As they prayed for me my back was healed, my leg was restored. I had faith to believe that the end result was going to be a complete healing, so it wasn't a surprise when it happened.

That's when I was called to live my life believing God for divine health and healing. I had experienced numerous healing touches prior to this call, once I knew that God was alive. God had shown himself to me through these incidences, that he could be trusted as my great Physician. I believed him, this has been my faith journey. You cannot expect to walk this way unless you have revelatory faith for it, but you can! I was just a young woman who believed God's word and took it seriously.

If we understand that we are one body with different functions and different levels of faith to do those functions, then I think it's safe to say we will not all do this. But let's just agree that it's a valid path in Christ. I find that I cannot talk about this way of living without someone almost challenging me with the defense of the medical profession. This does not mean that I have an issue with the medical profession! It's not a competition and it does not have to be faith vs. medicine. I know many Christians who believe in the power of healing, have been healed of various issues, and still see doctors.

Faith also takes obedience; it's obedience to each line upon line and precept upon precept. I was told by the Lord several years after that first directive, to fast one day a week for my health. He explained that it's like the tithe, I give him one day a week and he will take care of the rest. I do not have free rein over my body. He has coached me in sound wisdom all the way through. Recently, he told me to view sugar as poison, because sometimes I don't listen as well as I should! His wisdom profits anyone because he is not willing for any to perish for lack of knowledge. (Hosea 4:6)

The call to move to California was a faith thing as well. It started as a hard no in response, which was disobedience. Then over time I started asking him why, but he did not answer. Then I started verbalizing, "I wonder what he has for me out there?" I had no desire to leave my state. It was a process of letting go so I could see my path. I started feeling like the call to go was bubbling up inside of me until I had to say yes. It took seven years for me to say yes to that call. Through many details I won't include, I finally headed out there, white knuckling all the way!

Miracles happened on that trip, too. The tail lights of our rented truck had not been properly attached to the trailer that was carrying my car. But the brake lights worked anyway! This was confirmed at the time of the rental drop off. Also, the truck had a major leak in the transmission line, but the few quarts of fluid I added got us out there safely. God kept us safe when we had to pull over in Flagstaff because of a white out snowstorm. I had no idea we would need a room there. The only place with an opening was a flea bit motel, mainly used by construction and field workers coming to the area for work. It was quite late when we arrived, yet there were men still roaming the hotel corridors. We got a bed though, even if the heater in the room didn't work. He kept us safe through it all.

I had the outreach connections, support of the small church pastor that licensed me and the healing rooms pastor. However, once I got out there it wasn't really clear what I should do with my time. My first priority was to go out on the streets with the same outreach ministry I was associated with. When I did, I met up with friends from previous trips. Everyone was very encouraging about my new venture. But this one lady I knew was looking at me with a very strange expression. I asked her what was up and she said, "You're late." I asked her what she meant by that, since I had arrived to the outreach in plenty of time. She replied that I was late coming to California. She said the Lord had spoken to me to come over seven years ago and I should have obeyed right away. I knew this was a divine message, since she was speaking so accurately. I had not spoken to her in those seven years. I replied humbly that I was here now. She responded by saying that there were certain things put in place with obedience. All I could do was think about why it took me so long to say yes. I knew what she was saying was true. I needed to work on my obedience, to put God first so he could lead the way. I wanted his very best for me and for whomever he called me to serve. I repented for not obeying right away!

I couldn't afford to live in the city of San Francisco where the outreaches were centered, so I settled in a suburb of the East Bay. There I got involved in a church and met the pastor. This female pastor graciously introduced me around and I met one of my best friends. This new friend shared with me her conversion experience and it was almost identical to mine. To this day we are still best friends and sisters in the Lord. We talk on the phone pretty regular, but no matter how long it's been, we can get on the same page immediately. We have always run our race on the same parallel and I have learned so much from her!

My friend started bringing me to other church meetings and prayer groups where I often found myself sharing about the signs and wonders I'd experienced as a follower of Jesus. While I was doing a forty-day fast for where I should focus my attention, the Lord started opening up avenues for ministry much closer to my home. I also got involved with a group of intercessors that met together to pray and strategize by spiritual mapping. In 2002, while we were praying in a meeting, I prophesied that there was going to be a mass exodus leaving California. Twenty years later that prophecy is in full swing.

My favorite thing to do was being with my new friend, sharing in her circle of ministry opportunities. Sometimes we would volunteer at a women's shelter, sometimes help in the kitchen of a church holding a fundraising dinner, but we loved coming together to pray! These prayer meetings were a few hours, or over-nighters called "shut ins." One night at one of these meetings, the Lord clearly spoke to my heart that he would move me on from there. He said "The sowers of this field will reap this harvest." I found that to be a very sad word. He was giving me insight that he would lead me away from this area eventually. I thanked him for the warning. I was sad though because I knew my friend and I were going to part ways. A few days later I told her what the Lord said to me. We made a pact, that no matter where the Lord would lead us, we would keep in touch.

While doing the forty-day fast, I was given eyes to see that as individuals we are invited to enter the presence of the Lord, just as depicted in Psalm 100:4. It's like a map that guides us through a personal time of prayer and worship. We enter the presence of God the way Psalm 100:4 expresses; first go through his gates with thanksgiving, then his courtyard with praise. As we are brought closer, the closeness leads to an awareness of how unruly and unholy our human nature is, in light of a truly holy God! This leads to repentance, and when we are new to this, we may have a lot to repent for. Again, we are coming closer to a holy God. As we do this on a regular basis, the repentance becomes less woeful and more like a response. When we have unburdened ourselves of our sin, there is usually a silence, accompanied by an all-encompassing sense of peace. We have entered the atmosphere of our Lord! As we wait on him, we will be invited into his presence, the most holy place! This communion is meant for every born-again child of God, through the precious blood of Christ Jesus.

When Jesus rose from the grave and went to the Kingdom of God, he sat down at the right hand of the Most High, then he gave gifts to men. (Ephesians 4:8) The most precious gift Jesus gave to all believers was a literal "swapping" of his righteousness and dominance, to us on earth. He is there now, and in turn he gave us his full mantle here. We access the wisdom and knowledge of it all, according to our measure of faith and our gifts, by communing in the most holy place. That's where the Holy Spirit metes into our spirit, giving us understanding of whatever the Lord has for us. On any given occasion we can hear the Spirit whisper into our spirit, through bible reading, through prayer. But this is the place of true intimacy. I believe it's also where most of us will access healing.

This has been the map I have followed my entire walk. I can say for certain that by entering his presence, it has allowed the Lord to do the deepest healing and sanctification in me. It has caused great understanding in the written word of God as well. This is where the light in me sees the Light, where a convergence of his ways are imparted into my way of being. This is how I can put into action "I have been crucified with Christ; I no longer live. But the life that I now live, I live by faith in the son of God." (Galatians 2:20 paraphrased)

In light of this communing and as I relate it, I must also call attention to all of Ephesians, Chapter 4. This was my next insightful understanding of the body of Christ. I was given this understanding during the same fast and while I had been practicing Psalm 100:4. I saw that our great body, this living, breathing organism of Christ's, must see ourselves the way he sees us. Allow me to speak in a very blunt way so we can relate here. I see Ephesians 4:11-13, as an exhortation to become the unified body all together, to grow up and get on the same page. Then Christ Jesus can take his preeminent place at the top – as in a hierarchy.

And He Himself gave some *to be* apostles, some prophets, some evangelists, and some pastors and teachers, for the equipping of the saints for the work of ministry, for the edifying of the body of Christ, **until** we all come to the unity of the faith and of the knowledge of the Son of God, to a perfect man, to the measure of the stature of the fullness of Christ. (Ephesians 4:11-13 paraphrased)

My whole spirit felt this call, to see and do everything with this unique little word in mind: **until**. Personally, I don't think he will come back until we do what this passage says – grow up and get into our unique positions. Thereby we will be showing ourselves as mature, in unity and the knowledge of Christ.

Paul's letters are all one in the same, calling the body of Christ into unity and position. He is writing to the small cells of the church, expressing his sincere love, while exhorting them to love and serve one another. He is espousing the rule of the Kingdom, which is explained in Ephesians Chapter 4. We are one body, each with different functions and different degrees of faith, to carry out those functions and callings. We are not the same, though we are all one.

Imagine if I am the eye, but not just me. There are others in the body of Christ that have a type of a seer prophetic gift like me. I carry just one facet of this gift. I look around and I am united and supported by all the others around me. There are other entities around us, functioning in their perspective areas. I can see multi-millions of these like-minded servants operating this living organism, which turns out to be a body, while I look around from up there in the face.

Now I can easily understand that we operate like individual cells in the body of Christ, exactly like the human anatomy. We all work to make up and function this body. Likewise, when one cell goes off into delusions, it's like a cancer. Cancer usually spreads to other cells around it, and some cancers can jump. So, if the body of Christ has a brother or sister going off into a dark drama, we should have overwhelming consternation! It matters to us all whether our cells are healthy and functioning in accordance with the Holy Spirit, for we are one body!

To me, this picture also makes it clear that we cannot all be one of the five separate ministries, described as the fivefold, in Ephesians 4:11. These five positions are regulated in the body of Christ to be in authority over all the rest **until** we all become elevated into our positions. I say elevated because this is not where most of the body functions yet. They need to elevate their consciousness to align with who they are in Christ, in order to bring about our maturity. Therefore, they need to believe and accept their special gifts and talents that were bestowed upon each of us, when Christ sat down at the right hand of God in his heavenly place. (Ephesians 4:7-8)

Just as in the laws of nature, we are cells in a living, breathing dynamic called the body of Christ. No one cell is more important than the other. We carry our own set of properties and mass or structure, like an isotope. Isotopes are said to be stable, only if, when left alone they do not spontaneously change. It's so fitting to see why we need each other when you understand that at the very core of our designed nature, cells need each other in all ways. Even in fission – when atoms collide and tremendous energy is released, the result can be a controlled explosion of power. So again, when comparing the body of Christ to our most basic example of cells in nature, our coming together can ignite a spiritual power like no other on earth. Christ Jesus said the gates of hell cannot prevail against the church he will build! (Matthew 16:18)

Diamonds are formed from atoms, crystallized under intense heat and pressure. They rise to the surface of the earth through an eruption process. As the body of Christ, our shared understanding of kingdom principals can cause the rarest of stones to be developed out of us. By allowing the process of becoming transparent to our fellow believers and knowing them in the same way, we become like our head, the Chief Cornerstone. This is the principal foundation in our call to the assembly of the body of Christ. (1 Peter 2:4-8)

People are people, this is a difficult process. Iron sharpens iron, it's a pressure that you will have to endure. It's like the sinews of a muscle, tying it to the bone. As we choose the process of this pressure to refine us, the body gets stronger and stronger. If you let go of your own carnality, by repenting, and can see past others' carnality, you can share in a communal anointing! By seeing each other as greater, we extend to even the weakest what they need to be made strong. By sharing in a communal anointing, we have a reciprocation of each other's strengths and even our gifts. It's all for the kingdom, all for our maturing right up to the head, Christ Jesus!

We need to commune with Christ through the Holy Spirit because that's the glue holding us all together. It's where we will develop, starting with a healthy fear of God. The word **until** is contrasting a plan from the result. The plan is for our compliance with Christ's leadership. The result is a united priesthood having a perfect knowledge of what we possess in him. We must see that loving one another is part and parcel of manifesting the power of God in our lives.

There is a time coming, I believe very soon, when we will all get on the same page about who we are in Christ. When that happens, the world will have to take notice because of the corporate and individual power we will demonstrate! People will be healed and lives will turn completely around in an instant. The churches' growth will combust!

Chapter 8

Never Gonna be Without Him

While in California, I went from living in the East Bay area, to a suburb of Sacramento. I took a job in sales; a lucrative position and I liked talking with people. I needed work because while I was functioning as a minister, I wasn't getting paid. Once I left the bay area, I left those ministry opportunities behind too. Living in this new area allowed me to go to a church that was seeing the Holy Spirit move in their midst. Once I was at this church, I decided to go through their training course for more ministry opportunities in California.

While I was in training, I heard the Lord speak to me saying, "Your ministry is outside the four walls of the church. My church doesn't have walls." In my mind's eye I saw myself on the street, on any corner, ingratiating others with goodness so they would see that God is good! Then, as I pondered that, I saw how anything a Christian wants to do, they are bringing Christ into that circumstance. I saw how we are all a sea of humanity, all of us in need, all diamonds in the rough. As Christians, there isn't anywhere we go that we cannot find an outlet for our passion, our Savior!

Not long after he spoke this to me, that church lost their building. They weren't able to pay a balloon payment that had come due on the contract they signed. This was circa 2008. However, it positioned me to further realize that though I can be a member of a local church, my ministry would be outside the walls of the building.

In California my daughter finished high school and graduated with honors. While in her senior year, she met her future husband. My intention was to enroll her in college, then I was going to take my ministry desires further south in California. My daughter felt in her heart though that she wasn't cut out for a four-year college experience. Instead, she wanted to enroll in junior college, until she knew her course of study. I learned during this time that most young adults just graduating high school don't know what they should do; those who know are the exception. It wasn't easy for her, she went through course after course without a plan. She eventually let her part time job turn into full time work. She liked the field she was in and wanted to try other areas, which she did. While she did, she took night courses. This all led to her career path and a process of learning that has eventually made her a steady, great income! During all this, she got married.

I was living alone now, having a monstrous case of empty nest syndrome. My daughter and I had been so close, and people I knew had wondered out loud how having an empty nest was going to affect me. I didn't give it too much thought at the time. Now she was married and I had not felt this alone since before I had her. I had the Lord though, and he was ever present. I just didn't seem to get that right away. When I did, he spoke to me about going back home.

My folks were aging and I'd been saying how I'd like to go back and spend time with them before the inevitable happened. He heard me, and now he was asking me to go. He also knew I would not be able to obey until my darkest fear was brought to light. I was being asked to deal with a fear deep inside, my daughter's wellbeing. I would need to trust God with her, while she and her husband lived their new life together in California. I would be 2000 miles away.

On the day he asked me to trust him and deal with this fear, I became grief stricken by the loss of her. She was not gone, but the fear was so deep, the emotion of casting her over to him was like the grief of a death. It was within my gut and so very painful! I sobbed almost to convulsion until the pressure broke. In bent position on the floor, I finally had no more to cast out. I fell further down and rolled over on my back. It always amazes me when the Lord takes me to a place I didn't even know existed. There, finding a release after giving it to him, a new tangible freedom was given to me!

Then he instructed me to sell off everything but my most personal items. I was not taking the truckload of possessions that I had come with back again. He was asking me to clean it all out. I was amazed at his precise direction. If he said to list an item for thus amount, I'd question that it would go. Then the item would sell, for that amount in record time.

Since first moving to California, little by little most of my furniture had been given away or sold. It was my reality that possessions and even people were not to stop me from following Christ. I had been living out Luke 18:29-30 and John 12:24-26.

I moved back home to be with my family and I did what I could for them. This would be the first of three times that I went back and forth, from Minnesota to California. This first time coming home was the best within our family dynamic. I love Jesus so much! He had set me free from my past and I was gracefully able to be there with them.

Once back home, I felt drawn to prayer and communion. I spent many hours in a deep study of our position as Christ's bride. Then, while I was in prayer about this, I was given understanding of how a good marriage works. In marriage, the essence and energy of an individual is shared with the other. Each becomes part of the greater oneness of marriage. All that someone is, uniquely designed by God, all identity with self, becomes an extension of the married union. Because of this, getting rid of any negative self-image will produce a greater oneness, a greater marriage. As well, seeing ourself as God sees us will overcome any of the other person's shortcomings. Not seeing shortcomings negatively, but rather, what essence in one can eclipse or supplant that shortcoming, and actuate the other's growth? By using what each has to offer to bond, it will create a greater force. We bring what we can for the other person's balance, and vice versa. It was exactly how the body of Christ finds maturity!

Where most marriage struggles begin is by pointing out flaws, retaliating with an air of pride and feeling criticized. But don't see individual issues as negative. Instead, see that the overcoming quality is exactly what the other person brings to the union. This is for the greater benefit and allows oneness to be strengthened. It also allows each personhood to coexist within the marriage.

It's a choice to walk in a humbleness of spirit that allows these truths to prevail. Christ asks us to walk with him humbly and with a contrite heart, so he is able to flow in and through our lives. As I am open to him, I am constantly letting him eclipse my negative character issues of self. I am changed and become more like him.

In being back home, there have been relationships that were brought to an end, while others have been renewed on a much stronger foundation. I've also had my mind sharpened and my spirit renewed in ways that were not possible until now. I was a slow learner to the effects of fear. Now I don't live that way anymore. By living free of fear, it has uncovered more truth from God's written word, some of which he tried to expose me to before.

I know a few things now, and I don't doubt my own gifts and talents anymore. Being fully persuaded, I press on towards the goal of the high call of God in Christ Jesus! (Philippians 3:14a) To me, this verse means so much. I am fully persuaded that we have the same authority that Christ does! Being Spirit filled believers, we now take his place here, and are recipients of his mantle of authority in our unique positions. I've also learned to speak into my atmosphere what I hear him say. He is the author and perfector of my faith! (Hebrews 12:2)

My belief rests in the fact that God will be mastering a perfected bride until he takes her away. I believe the bride of Christ will be set apart on earth until this reunion with her husband. This means that she will be given all things to be beautiful to a lost and dying world; she will have the answers!

It's also a very beautiful world that we live in, that he created. So, I live a purposeful life of taking in his awesome creation around me. Once, in an early morning conversation I had with the Lord, I asked him if he had any favorites during his time on earth. He answered me back clearly. Along with other things, he said he liked looking up at a blue sky, just like I do. I was totally surprised! His next comment implied a question; why was I surprised? He said he likes the color blue, after all, he created it. I still chuckle as I remember that.

Matthew 25:1-13 describes a set of ten virgins that were awaiting their husband whom they were properly engaged to. Five waited in earnest, making sure that even if he came at night, they would be ready. They had filled the oil in their lamps, keeping it topped off. These five did indeed prepare properly, for their betrothed came in the middle of the night. They were whisked off to happiness!

The other five were not prepared, did not show that this intended arrival was important to them. They ended up begging to be with him, banging on the door of his home. But he said he wasn't going to let them in, that he didn't know them after all. Ouch!

It's pretty clear to me from this passage that some are going to be ready for Christ's return, and some are not. Think of it, the same church body, but some will not enter into his kingdom. That is truly scary to me. I didn't find out about him to be left without a home to share with him! I explained in the beginning of sharing my journey, that once I found out he was real and he was alive, I was hot on his trail. I wasted no time finding out how to get closer! I'm still that person, wanting to experience everything he has to show me, right up until the day he calls for me. I'm not holding back anymore. I am in constant prayer for our body to become mature in its highest purpose and goal! I write with hope that you are likeminded in this regard. Leave everything behind, lay your life on the line. There is nothing more valuable on earth.

Chapter 9

Conclusion

God can't do what?! There isn't anything he can't do! I have seen time and time again that he can be trusted to heal me, to tangibly lead me through difficulties and new experiences, to recreate me. He is ever present and he restores my soul every time I reach out to commune with him. He loves to commune with us and is always present when we make ourselves available. He can and he will change you too, into a rare and precious living being, with a purpose that he always intended for you! He does it every day, to lives that we don't hear about or see. Regardless whether we see or know them, he knows them! And they are powerful when they are conformed to his will.

If you've picked up this book and after reading it, you have been convinced that the world has no good answers for you and you are lost, then read a bit further. I want you to know that you are a pearl of great price the Lord came to earth to purchase with his own life, by dying on the cross! He wanted you to search him out and find the truth. I want you to know that he did it all for a treasure like you! You were created by him and he always had a purpose and a plan for you. I am living proof of this.

He rose again to show us that his kingdom exists and we have been given all we need, our precious engagement ring, the Holy Spirit! I promise you, if you take the next steps, he will lead you, guide you and never leave you. The Holy Spirit will see to it, he sticks closer than a brother.

As best as you can, speak out to him that you have been wrong about many things, and you are sorry. You can list what you know are sins. Then tell him that you are ready to let him take the steering wheel of your life. You can tell him that you are choosing to let him lead and you will learn to hear his voice and listen to what he tells you. He does speak and you will learn to hear him! (John 10:1-5) Then love him with all you got! Because you will learn that you can never be removed from him when you do.

Don't get frustrated with your process, your journey. As I described, it can be tough in the beginning because you are being recreated in the image of Christ. Just don't run from him if or when you go backwards, no matter how guilty or shameful you feel. Those are not his feelings for you! That's your enemy, the very one that has contributed to your lost self. Jesus won't be surprised because he knows the beginning from the end. His own words say that it's a growth. But you will need to help yourself by getting a bible that you can read. I recommend a modern-day translation. I would have you consider the New King James version, the New Living Translation or the Amplified bibles. Also, have a concordance available in book or app form and learn to use it. It's quite simple and this will help you find out the root meaning of words regarding topics he shows you.

Don't think that you can juxtapose your lifestyle without help and support. You will need the church; we all need the church! We are one and the same, different parts of a big body. We are all his and must come together in this resolve. Find a church that welcomes newcomers, but also teaches directly from God's written word, the bible. Don't be concerned about what you are supposed to be or do. He has you now, he is the author and perfector of your faith! In all ways, we are all growing up into him. But keep in mind that tiny little word, **until.**

Peace in Christ Jesus!

About the Author

Leslie Ann lives in Minnesota at the time of this book release. Since being Spirit filled, Leslie has been a true Jesus freak with no apologies. Her passion for creative expression is only surpassed by her determination to share her faith. She raised her daughter alone and to date has not married.

Leslie stays in touch with her mentors, as well as her oldest friends in Christ. Always putting one on one time first, she cherishes her relationships with family and friends. She still allows the Lord to dictate her health and lifestyle. She is ever hopeful to see the return of the Lord in her lifetime!

The book cover art is a painting by Leslie, captioned, "Faith is the equivalent of sunshine; we need it to grow." In the painting, her creative take on a sunflower bends and breathes in the glow of the sun, much like us as we worship in God's presence.

The title of this book comes from a poem Leslie wrote as she struggled to obtain freedom from inner bondages. It's a cry to God, to wholly consume her and cover her with His merciful love.

If you would like more information, please email
response360degrees@gmail.com.
Thank you for your interest!